BIRMINGHAM REVOLUTIONARIES

BIRMINGHAM REVOLUTIONARIES

The Reverend Fred Shuttlesworth and the
Alabama Christian Movement for Human Rights

Edited By

MARJORIE L. WHITE & ANDREW M. MANIS

Mercer University Press
Macon, Georgia

ISBN 0-86554-709-2   MUP/H530

The paper used in this publication meets the minimum requirements of American National Standard for Information Sciences—Permanence of Paper for Printed Library Materials, ANSI Z39.48-1984.

"The Historical Significance of Birmingham" originally published in Wyatt T. Walker, *Millennium End Papers* (New York: Martin Luther King Fellows Press, 2000). Reprinted with permission.

"A Fire You Can't Put Out: The Meaning of Fred Shuttlesworth and His Movement" by Andrew Manis is a distillation of the author's book *A Fire You Can't Put Out: The Civil Rights Life of Birmingham's Reverend Fred Shuttlesworth* (Tuscaloosa: University of Alabama Press, 1999), and is used here with permission of the University of Alabama Press.

Library of Congress Cataloging-in-Publication Data

Marjorie L. White and Andrew M. Manis, eds.
     Birmingham Revolutionaries: The Reverend Fred Shuttlesworth and the Alabama Christian Movement for Human Rights / Marjorie L. White and Andrew M. Manis, eds.
         p. cm.
Collection of essays presented at a symposium entitled Brimingham revolutionaries: the Reverend Fred Shuttlesworth and the Alabama Christian movement for human rights, held in Birmingham in November 1998.
Includes bibliographical references.
     ISBN 0-86554-709-2 (alk. paper)
1. Shuttlesworth, Fred L., 1922---Congresses. 2. Civil Rights movements--Alabama--Birmingham--History--20th century--Congresses. 3. Afro-Americans--Civil rights--Alabama--Birmingham--History--20th century--Congresses. 4. Civil rights workers--Alabama--Birmingham--Biography--Congresses. 5. Birmingham (Ala.)--Race relations--Congresses. 6. Alabama Christian Movement for Human Rights--Congresses.
I. White, Marjorie Longenecker. II. Manis, Andrew Michael.

F334.B69 N425 2000
305.8'960730761781--dc21   00-63822

CONTENTS

PREFACE

Marjorie L. White

The need, the great need, now is for people to understand how and why the movement began and what happened and how it happened and what they had to go through.
—The Reverend Fred Shuttlesworth at a mass meeting, Bethel Baptist Church, November 2, 1998

On the short list of the most important historical events of twentieth century American history are the civil rights demonstrations of April and May 1963 in Birmingham, Alabama. These protests, which resulted in the use of police dogs and fire hoses against marchers, attracted worldwide attention and eventually led to the passage of the Civil Rights Act of 1964, national legislation protecting the constitutional rights of African-Americans and other minority groups.

The conventional view in the news media and in popular historical memory is that the Birmingham protests were the work of "outside agitators": Martin Luther King Jr. and the Southern Christian Leadership Conference (SCLC). This view also holds that Birmingham ("Bombingham" as it was known to some) was an evil place held up to a mirror by King, who used the principles of nonviolence and civil disobedience to make a point to the nation and the world.

These pages present a different interpretation: the Birmingham protests were primarily the work of a blue collar, faith-based movement built, not in a month or a year, but over seven difficult years around a network of humble Birmingham churches whose pastors and people placed their faith in God and their lives and those of their children in his hands, while they destroyed the old order. In this view, the events of April and May 1963 in Birmingham were a triumph of Birmingham people, a triumph to be celebrated, not bemoaned.

Martin Luther King Jr. did not initiate the events of the spring of 1963 and he was not the primary actor in the critical years leading up to that time. Instead, King was invited to Birmingham by the Reverend Fred Shuttlesworth, secretary of the SCLC and leader of the Alabama Christian Movement for Human Rights (ACMHR), an independent organization often affiliated with the SCLC. Shuttlesworth's invitation was resisted by moderate, middle-class elements in Birmingham's black community, who supported subsequent demonstrations only after the national spotlight was turned on.

King's role in Birmingham was undeniably of great importance, and his ability to give voice to the dreams and aspirations of African Americans and to their righteous claim to equal treatment in American society are deserving of the honors the received and the esteem in which he is held. The pragmatic decision of Shuttlesworth and the other Birmingham leaders to subordinate their roles to that of King as national spokesman for their cause was undoubtedly in the best interests of the civil rights movement. However, it was Shuttlesworth who held King's feet (and those of everyone else) to the fire and forced the uncompromising stand in Birmingham that stimulated such a strong reaction from around the world, placing the movement firmly on the road to success.

The essays in this volume by Glenn Eskew, Wilson Fallin, Jr., Andrew Manis, Aldon Morris, and Wyatt Tee Walker were initially presented at a symposium entitled *Birmingham Revolutionaries: The Reverend Fred Shuttlesworth and the Alabama Christian Movement for Human Rights*. The symposium was held in Birmingham in November 1998 on the occasion of the publication of the Birmingham Historical Society's pictorial chronology of the Birmingham movement, *A Walk to Freedom: The Reverend Fred*

Shuttlesworth and the Alabama Christian Movement for Human Rights, 1956-1964.

A *Walk to Freedom* and this collection of addresses tell the story of the Birmingham movement from the perspective of the local movement. In these pages, action takes place within the context of the African-American church, a network of ultimately sixty churches spread across the length and breadth of the industrial city. The Birmingham movement met every Monday night, beginning June 5, 1956, and every night in times of crises and testing of segregation laws. Most meeting churches were small to medium sized structures located in blue-collar neighborhoods adjacent to heavy industrial plants. ACMHR headquarters was at Bethel Baptist Church, home church to the Reverend Fred Shuttlesworth. As the ACMHR grew, members recruited larger churches, particularly those in the city center where sit-ins, protests, and boycotts began in 1960 and culminated in the mass demonstrations of April and May 1963.

The Birmingham movement is a remarkable story of people of stalwart faith who believed that God would help them in their all-out, nonviolent effort to banish segregation. Participants in the movement took extraordinary risks, believing that God would keep them safe or that the principles they fought for justified following the example of Christ's ultimate sacrifice. They walked together, endured and suffered together, until freedom was won for all Americans through the passage of the Civil Rights Act of 1964.

Beginning in 1993, the Birmingham Historical Society, working at times with the Historic American Engineering Record (HAER) and the Historic American Building Survey (HABS), both documentation branches of the National Park Service based in Washington, DC, conducted field work and archival research that resulted in histories, large-format photographs, and measured drawings of several significant Birmingham civil rights churches and the mapping of others. (National Park Service studies of 600 Birmingham historic sites, conducted in 1992 and 1993, had pointed to the "national significance" of the Birmingham move-ment.) Full HABS documentation was completed by 1996 for the working-class Bethel Baptist Church of Collegeville, which had been led by Shuttlesworth and was home base for the ACMHR, and the Sixteenth Street Baptist Church, the large and centrally located middle-class church that was the staging point for major marches, but better known for the infamous bombing that killed four young girls on September 15, 1963. The Society conducted additional field surveys and archival research identifying movement era churches and their use for the regular Monday mass meetings and as strategy and training centers. In 1996, documentation consultant Richard Anderson of Sumter, South Carolina mapped the movement churches for the Historical American Engineering Record, locating the churches on a 1962 land use and zoning map of the city.

The Society currently seeks National Register of Historic Places status for the Birmingham movement churches and other associated sites as well as National Historic Landmark status for the Bethel and Sixteenth Street Baptist.[1] Former ACMHR secretary Lola Hendricks and Birmingham Civil Rights Institute President Emerita Odessa Woolfolk helped identify and research the sixty movement churches and associated sites to be considered for nomination. Many other individuals, especially Fred Shuttlesworth, Colonel Stone Johnson and Wilson Fallin Jr., assisted with research and preparation of reports and publications.

---

[1]The National Register of Historic Places, established in 1996, is the nation's official list of properties worthy of preservation. Properties listed can be of local, state and national significance. National Historic Landmarks, established 1935, are "the most significant places in American history—they illustrate and commemorate our collective past and help us understand our national identity. National Historic Landmarks outstandingly represent and interpret the best and brightest and the most tragic aspects of our history. Through these Landmarks, all Americans can better understand and appreciate the broad trends and events, important persons, great ideas and ideals, and valuable accomplishments in the arts and sciences, and humanities, that are truly significant in our history." Robert G. Stanton, Director, National Park Service, writing in the preface to the National Register Bulletin: *How to Prepare National Historic Landmark Nominations*, 1999.

Historians at National Landmarks (a Washington, D.C. branch of the National Park Service) reviewed preliminary documentation on the Bethel and Sixteenth Street Baptist Churches in 1996 and directed a National Landmark nomination to proceed for the Sixteenth Street church *only*. They failed to find in Shuttlesworth and his organization "the extraordinary national significance" required for conferring National Historic Landmark status on the Bethel Baptist Church site.

The Birmingham Historical Society published *A Walk to Freedom: The Reverend Fred Shuttlesworth and the Alabama Christian Movement for Human Rights, 1956-1964* and organized the *Birmingham Revolutionaries* symposium to gather together scholars and other participants whose reflections would build a case for the national significance of Shuttlesworth and the local Birmingham movement.

Shuttlesworth objected to the use of the term "revolutionaries" in describing movement members, due to the movement's insistence on nonviolence. However, a revolution, defined as a "drastic change in a government or social system," did take place. Both local and national laws and government structures changed as a result of the nonviolent protests in Birmingham. The Alabama Humanities Foundation provided major funding for the symposium held November 2, 1998 at the Sixteenth Street Baptist Church and for the old-fashioned mass meeting held that evening at Bethel.

A significant element of the historical interpretation shared by the essays delivered at the symposium is the role of religion and the churches in the freedom struggle. Historians such as David Garrow and Taylor Branch have underscored this theme as it pertains to the life and thought of Martin Luther King Jr. All participants at the symposium emphasized this theme, with particular attention to Shuttlesworth's activism. Though King's interest in Gandhian nonviolence and other forms of social philosophy have occasionally led interpreters to give his religious background less attention than it deserved, such would be impossible in a study of Shuttlesworth's thought and involvement.

Unre-servedly religious, Shuttlesworth is more preacher than historian, and never fails to attribute the movement's success to the Almighty. Consider Shuttlesworth's comments as, during the 1998 mass meeting, he once again stood at the pulpit of Bethel Baptist Church. "God," he said with absolute conviction, "chose this spot, this sacred church."

The civil rights conflict in Birmingham was not, as some believe, a mistake. It was the result of disciplined, principled, and strategically brilliant action by a network of inspired, working-class, churchgoing people led by their pastors. Neither is the conflict a cause for shame. Rather, it is to be celebrated as a magnificent achievement of the human spirit. Few times in our history has a group of ordinary men and women risked life and limb so unremittingly for the purpose of achieving liberty and equality. Birmingham can be proud that its citizens won their *revolutionary* fight for freedom on its streets.

INTRODUCTION

Andrew M. Manis

Only those historians or journalists with stubbornly secular worldviews can fail to appreciate the deep religiousness of the American civil rights movement. If that is true of the segment of the black freedom struggle centered on Martin Luther King Jr., it is all the more applicable to the Birmingham movement. This is indicated by the participation of the sixty "movement churches" documented by the Birmingham Historical Society, the high percentage of church membership among the membership of the Alabama Christian Movement for Human Rights, and especially the Christian activism of Fred Shuttlesworth.[1]

Birmingham's indigenous "civil rights preacher" was indeed, as Marjorie White has noted, "unreservedly religious." Even when talking about repairing an automobile Shuttlesworth brings "the Lord" into the discussion. I suspect one reason why Shuttlesworth's name is little known outside the circle of civil rights participants and historians is that his deep religious consciousness and vocabulary were so off-putting to the secularly-oriented news media that first reported on the movement in the 1950s and 1960s. Though just as religious as Shuttlesworth, the more educated and polished Martin Luther King Jr. could speak to

---

[1]On the religiosity of the ACMHR membership, see Jacquelyne Johnson Clarke, "Goals and Techniques in Three Civil Rights Organizations in Alabama" (Ph.D. diss., Ohio State University, 1960).

media types in the language of economics and social philosophy. By contrast, Shuttlesworth tended to explain the movement, and especially his own role in it, in a traditional "God language" that marked him as much less urbane than King. His calling into the ministry, his vocation into civil rights activism, his numerous escapes from segregationist violence, and his victories in the freedom struggle were always credited to divine guidance.

But unlike Shuttlesworth and other ministerial participants in the movement, historians cannot hold such a view. However religious they may be at a personal level, historians must nevertheless look for human agency and activity in social movements like the black freedom struggle. They cannot say clearly that God acted in a certain way at a certain time; they can—and in this case *must*—say that they the human actors *believed* that God acted in or through their actions. They can and must also say that Shuttlesworth and his followers were children of Christian faith. They must say that the fire that blazed undiminished by Birmingham's fire hoses in 1963 was lit in the hearth of the city's African-American churches. This perspective is shared by all of the voices heard in this volume.

In the first essay, historian Wilson Fallin Jr. puts the civil rights movement in the long, historical context of the black churches of Birmingham. He emphasizes the "rock solid faith" built into these churches from Birmingham's beginnings as a city to the beginning of the civil rights movement. He samples the sermons, prayers, and leadership styles of Birmingham's African-American congregations, showing how church culture gave birth to and was reflected in the city's indigenous civil rights activism.

Next, sociologist Aldon D. Morris, author of the influential study, *The Origins of the Civil Rights Movement,* addresses a number of important issues around the framework of the importance of local movement for sustaining the civil rights fight. Like Fallin and all of other symposium presenters, Morris highlights the importance of the black church. He argues that because of national and international attention to the 1963 protests, the Birmingham movement struck a blow "heard 'round the world" and was indispensable to the success of the national civil rights movement. More specifically, he emphasizes the role of Fred Shuttlesworth in instilling in his followers the courage to confront "Bull" Connor and segregationist structures in Birmingham. This he did through radically confrontational acts of courage, which in turn convinced "people who had been beaten down by centuries of oppression, that they could use the method of direct action to confront their enemy."

In the third essay, Glenn T. Eskew sketches a clear picture of the class tensions that Fred Shuttlesworth and his movement generated in Birmingham's black community. Here Eskew distills one of the key arguments of his important book, *But for Birmingham: The Local and the National Movements in the Civil Rights Struggle,* winner of the 1999 Francis B. Simkins Award of the Southern Historical Association. He highlights the conflict between Shuttlesworth, a young preacher fairly new to Birmingham's black ministerial circles, and older, established pastors of the city's most prominent middle-class black churches. In particular he outlines the resentments of the Reverend J. L. Ware, pastor of the Trinity Baptist Church and president of the Birmingham Ministers' Conference, and the Reverend Luke Beard, leader of the Sixteenth Street Baptist Church. Eskew shows how the civil rights movement in Birmingham was a *working class movement* and headquartered not in the more prestigious Sixteenth Street church, but rather in Shuttlesworth's Bethel Baptist Church.

My own contribution to this volume focuses on the meanings of Fred Shuttlesworth and his movement. Most significantly, the essay argues that Shuttlesworth's work in Birmingham, both in the 1963 demonstrations and in the seven years of preparatory activism leading up to them, was indispensable to the success of not only the Birmingham movement, but to the civil rights movement as a whole. Put very bluntly, Fred Shuttlesworth has not received the credit he deserves for his role in the civil rights movement. Birmingham was crucial to the Civil Rights Act of 1964. Without Fred Shuttlesworth there would have been no Birmingham movement. In addition, the essay highlights the undiluted blackness, courage, and African-American spirituality of the Birmingham leader and his followers.

One of the most important leaders of the civil rights movement, Wyatt T. Walker, makes a powerful argument for "the historical significance of Birmingham." Uniquely qualified to provide both historical reminiscence and scholarly analysis, Walker was executive director of King's Southern Christian Leadership Conference (SCLC) during the 1963 demonstrations, which he dubbed "Project C (Confrontation)." In that capacity, he was assigned the responsibility to draw up the strategies and tactics for the protests. Surveying the territory in Birmingham with the help of Shuttlesworth and other local activists, Walker both planned and executed the specific activities of the marchers. This perspective makes Walker's essay all the more telling, as he views Birmingham as the most important chapter of the entire civil rights struggle. In addition, he connects Birmingham with Selma. He argues that the Birmingham protests rescued King and the SCLC from its most humiliating defeat in Albany, Georgia and set the stage for the Selma campaign, which precipitated the Voting Rights Act of 1965.

Finally, the volume concludes with the reminiscences of the Reverend Fred Shuttlesworth himself. Still alive and well at seventy-eight years of age as of this writing, the long-time pastor and social activist reflects on the divine role in the success of the movement. Self-styled as "a fighter, not a writer," Shuttlesworth himself has written comparatively little on these matters. Often interviewed and invited to speak at events marking the Martin Luther King Jr. Holiday, Shuttlesworth provides a vintage statement of the this-worldly piety that propelled him into the freedom struggle, into a prophetic ministry related to justice issues, and into a more traditional pastoral ministry.

All of these essays focus on the same movement from slightly different vantage points and highlighting different facets. As they derive from addresses delivered at a public event, they necessarily suffer from some repetition as to the narrative of events. In order, however, to honor the integrity of the original addresses at the

Birmingham Revolutionaries Symposium, they remain intact as delivered, without editing out the occasional redundancies. Footnotes have also been added for scholars and other readers of these essays.

What these essays have in common, of course, is great respect for the sixty civil rights churches that provided a "shelter in time of storm" for the Birmingham revolutionaries whose actions and impact are discussed in these pages. The authors provide these perspectives in eager hope that eventually the contributions of Fred Shuttlesworth and his followers in Birmingham will be properly appreciated.

1

ROCK SOLID FAITH:
AFRICAN-AMERICAN CHURCH LIFE AND CULTURE IN 1956 BIRMINGHAM

Wilson Fallin Jr.

The civil rights movement in Birmingham cannot be understood apart from the African-American church. Although there had been protest in Birmingham prior to 1956, a mass-based movement of direct action did not come into being until the formation of the Alabama Christian Movement for Human Rights, a movement of churches and pastors.

To understand the power and activism of the church that was unleashed in Birmingham in the 1950s and 1960s, especially with the formation of the ACMHR in 1956, it is necessary to take a brief look at the history and functions that the African-American church filled in the city. The city of Birmingham was founded in 1871 and soon became the industrial city of the New South. Blacks who were suffering under the vicious system of sharecropping in the Black Belt of South Alabama began to move into the city in the 1870s seeking better economic opportunity. After erecting or finding homes, they immediately began to form churches. The church had been the central institution in the Black

Belt communities from which these African Americans had come. In these communities, church worship was characterized by emotional fervor with lively singing, preaching, and praying. In the Black Belt these churches also served as the social and educational centers, with the pastor as the leader. Wooden church buildings with pot belly stoves were found all over South Alabama.[1]

Moving into Birmingham, African-American migrants established churches in every area of the city and county, which resembled those which had existed in the Black Belt from which they came. Churches were established in mining camps, adjacent cities and towns, in company villages, and in the inner city of Birmingham. Churches were started under brush arbors, in homes, and in store fronts. Some in back alleys, others on main streets. Many began as prayer meetings and Bible studies. Several emerged as the result of revivals. Others were the result of missionary activities by denominations.[2]

Wherever or however they were formed, churches in Birmingham immediately became centers of community life for the migrants. Churches helped black migrants adjust and accommodate to the strange new life of the city. These churches also exercised moral discipline by expelling those members found guilty of moral offenses.[3]

Most of all, African-American churches were the spiritual institutions that met the religious needs of blacks in the city.

---

[1]Malcolm C. McMillan, *Yesterday's Birmingham* (Miami: Seaman Publishing, Inc., 1957), 9-38; Leah Atkins, *The Valley and the Hills: An Illustrated History of Birmingham* (Woodland Hills, California: Windsor Publications, Inc., 1981), 50-61; Charles S. Johnson, *Shadow of the Plantation* (Chicago: University of Chicago Press, 1969), 154-156; Glen Sisk, "Negro Churches in the Alabama Black Belt, 1875-1900," *Journal of Presbyterian Historical Society* XXXIII (June 1955), 87-88.

[2]WPA Church Records of Alabama Churches found in the Alabama Archives Montgomery, Alabama, Boxes 44-46.

[3]Wilson Fallin, Jr., *The African American Church in Birmingham, Alabama, 1815-1963: A Shelter in the Storm* (New York: Garland Publishing, Inc., 1997), 48; Edward Wheeler, *Uplifting the Race: The Black Minister in the New South, 1865-1902* (New York: University Press of America, 1982), 80.

Given only the dirtiest and most unskilled jobs, relegated to the worst housing areas and viewed by whites as inferior, African Americans found little in the wider community to give them worth, dignity, and self-esteem. The church was the one place blacks could feel good about themselves. They were deacons, trustees, ushers, choir members, and heads of organizations. In the church they were somebody and respected. As a spiritual institution, the church was the place where African Americans could go and escape the hostility of the white world in Birmingham. There they could express their deepest thoughts and highest hopes. Key to black self-esteem, hope, and self-respect was the preaching of their pastors. Through sermons such as "Moses at the Red Sea," "Dry Bones in the Valley," and "The Eagle Stirreth Her Nest," blacks could identify their plight with the Old Testament Israelites and knew that God was working on their behalf.[4]

African Americans continued to arrive in the city of Birmingham so that by 1890 they comprised forty percent of the population. By that date there were twenty-seven "colored" churches listed in the Birmingham City Directory with countless others in the county and other adjacent areas. As African Americans continued to move into the city, the church served not only their moral and spiritual needs but was also in the forefront of establishing institutions to meet their physical and secular needs in a segregated city. As the central institution in the community, churches supported and enhanced the other institutions established by blacks. Because of the unique role of pastors in the churches, they became the key leaders in the wider community. Using their churches as a base, they established institutions to fill the economic, educational, and welfare needs of African Americans in the city. For example, the Reverend William R. Pettiford, pastor of the Sixteenth Street Baptist Church in 1865 founded the first black bank in the city which provided the funds for black home

---

[4]Robert J. Norrell, *The Other Side: The Story of Birmingham's Black Community* (Birmingham, n.d.), no. pg.; Keith Miller, *Voices of Deliverance: The Language of Martin Luther King, Jr. and its Sources* (New York: The Free Press, 1992), 23-26.

ownership and the many black businesses established in the city between 1890 and 1914. In 1894, the Reverend T. W. Walker, pastor of the Shiloh Baptist Church, and an associate of Pettiford, established the first standard insurance company in the city, the Union Central Relief Association.[5]

Although Pettiford and Walker and other pastors in Birmingham did not make a frontal assault to destroy the system of legal segregation, they criticized and petitioned against what they saw as the abuses of the Jim Crow system in Birmingham. After World War II, pastors became more vocal and assertive. They worked with laymen in the NAACP, which petitioned for the right to vote and the elimination of job discrimination. The Reverend R. L. Alford served as president of the NAACP with other pastors serving as vice-presidents and chairpersons for key committees. Several pastors in their sermons and addresses called for the end of segregation and all racial injustices. Mass meetings calling for the end to all forms of discriminations were held in churches.[6]

By 1956, the African-American church and its pastors were in the best position to project a mass-based, direct action movement. By that year there were at least 400 African-American churches in Birmingham and the county, located in every African-American community. These churches touched everybody in one way or another, the masses and the middle class. There was a common church culture that united these churches. Like all African-American church communities, there were different denominations, open conflicts, and social distinctions, but these differences did not destroy the common features that existed. For example,

---

[5]James V. Harris, "Reforms in Government Control of Negroes Birmingham, Alabama, 1890-1920," *Journal of Southern History* (November 1972), 571; Booker T. Washington, *The Negro in Business* (Boston: Hertel, Jenkins and Company, 1907), 113-114; Isabel Dangaix Allen, "Negro Enterprise: An Institutional Church," *Outlook* (September 1904), 180-183.

[6]Fallin, *African American Church in Birmingham*, 73; Martha Bigelow Mitchell, "Birmingham: Biography of a City of the New South," (Ph.D. dissertation: University of Chicago, 1946), 105; *Birmingham News*, December 20, 1895; *Birmingham World*, January 12, 1952.

practically all African-American churches sang the same songs; spirituals, gospels, and meter hymns. "Jesus Keep Me Near the Cross," "We are Climbing Jacob's Ladder," "The Lord Will Make a Way Somehow," and "When I Can Read My Title Clear" were common in practically all churches. Long and fervent prayers were a part of church services. The minister was a charismatic figure who was expected to preach with emotion and power, and to elicit a response and a loud chorus of Amens. These songs, prayers, and the preaching of the pastor expressed the hopes and aspirations of an oppressed people who desired freedom and equal rights.

From the worship in their churches blacks received a rock solid faith that not only sustained them, but gave them courage to form a civil rights movement. Their faith proved to them that right was stronger than wrong, truth was stronger than lies, and God's power was greater than the devil's. Most of all, they were convinced that God would be with them and help them to overcome the segregation in Birmingham.[7]

In addition to the common faith of the churches, pastors were generally respected and had a history of leadership in the community. These pastors had formed minister's conferences and other organizations where they had learned to cooperate and to engage in common activities. For example, the Birmingham Baptist Ministers' Conference had a membership of over 200 ministers. There was also the Interdenominational Ministerial Alliance, and the Methodist Ministers' Alliance.[8]

In 1956, a group of churches and pastors, assisted by a group of laywomen and laymen, formed a movement to free blacks from the oppression and rigid segregation that existed in the city. The outlawing of the NAACP in Alabama was the spark that set off this

---

[7]Aldon Morris, *The Origin of the Civil Rights Movement: Black Communities Organizing for Change* (New York: Free Press, 1984), 1-76. The figure of four hundred churches was garnered from Baptist associations and Methodist conference records. The City Directory was also helpful but did not include all African-American churches in the Birmingham area.

[8]Fallin, *African American Church in Birmingham*, 144.

mass-based movement in Birmingham. The NAACP had been the chief organization in promoting school integration and other anti-segregation practices in the state after the *Brown* decision of 1954.[9]

One person perturbed by the ban of the NAACP was the Reverend Fred Shuttlesworth, pastor of the Bethel Baptist Church. He proposed a mass meeting to see if African Americans in Birmingham wanted to organize to fight for their rights. He convinced six pastors to join him in the call.[10]

They announced the rally over the radio and in the city's black newspaper, the *Birmingham World,* scheduling the meeting for June 5, 1956, at the Sardis Baptist Church. More than a thousand people overflowed the church. The meeting resembled a tent revival, with Shuttlesworth as "the featured evangelist." "The actions of the Attorney General make it more necessary that Negroes come together in their own interest and plan together for the furtherance of their cause," as Shuttlesworth maintained. He warned the audience that the "citizen's council won't like this, but then I don't like a lot of things they do." Shuttlesworth continued: "Our citizens are restive under the yoke of segregation. . . . The only thing we are interested in is uniting our people in seeing that the laws of the land are upheld according to the Constitution of the United States."

The crowd responded with "Amen," "That's right," and "Yes, yes," as if they were in an African-American revival. Although a few ministers who had been longtime leaders in the community spoke against the formation of the organization, the audience voted three times to adopt the recommendations of Shuttles-

---

[9]Fred Shuttlesworth, "An Account of the Alabama Christian Movement for Human Rights," in Jacqueline Johnson Clarke, *These Rights They Seek: The Comparison of the Goals and Techniques of Local Civil Rights Organizations* (Washington, DC: Public Affairs Press, 1962), 135-139; Glen Thomas Eskew, "The Alabama Christian Movement and the Birmingham Struggle, 1956-1963" (M.A. thesis: University of Georgia, 1987), 5-9.

[10]Shuttlesworth, "An Account of the ACMHR," 136-139; Anne Braden, "The History That We Made in Birmingham, 1956-1979," *Southern Exposure* 7 (Summer 1979), 50-51.

worth's group and form the Alabama Christian Movement for Human Rights (ACMHR).[11]

An important feature of the Birmingham movement and the ACMHR was the central role of Fred Shuttlesworth. Shuttlesworth possessed a stubborn will, indomitable faith, and a sense of divine compulsion and destiny. He felt that God had called him to the task of destroying segregation in Birmingham. A core of approximately fifteen pastors surrounded Shuttlesworth, forming the ACMHR inner circle. They supported the movement financially and with their attendance, served on the board of directors, and were dedicated to Shuttlesworth's leadership. The parishioners of these pastors' churches made up the bulk of the membership of the organization.[12]

In almost every way the ACMHR mirrored the African-American church and its culture. Its leader was a charismatic figure in a pastoral mode who believed God had called him for the task. His followers also believed in his divine calling and would show their esteem for his leadership by standing and applauding as he entered the mass meetings. The ACMHR board of directors resembled a board of deacons. They met infrequently, at Shuttlesworth's request, and he essentially made all the decisions. The group raised funds through its membership dues, but also as in most African-American churches, it raised money by taking offerings at mass meetings and special events such as suppers, teas, musicals, and candy and bake sales. Each year the ACMHR observed an anniversary celebration which resembled the anniversary celebrations which were common in African-American churches. It was a way of fund-raising and celebrating the achieve-

---

[11]*Birmingham News*, June 6, 1956; Shuttlesworth, "An Account of the ACMHR," 139-140.

[12]Glenn T. Eskew, "The Alabama Movement for Human Rights, 1956-1963" in David Garrow, ed., *Birmingham, Alabama, 1956-1963* (Brooklyn, New York: Carlson Publishing Company, 1989), 70; Interview with Fred Shuttlesworth, January 25, 1993.

ments of the organization, with President Shuttlesworth giving his yearly report.[13]

As in every African-American church, the ACMHR had its own choir and ushers. Twenty-three members of the organization formed the ACMHR choir in July, 1960 at the Forty-Sixth Street Baptist Church. W. E. Shortridge, treasurer of the ACMHR, and Mrs. Georgia Price, an active laywoman, inspired its formation. Shortridge saw it as a way of enhancing the spirituality of the Monday night meetings. Its first organist was Nathaniel Lee, but in 1960 Carlton Reese became the director, song arranger, writer, and organist for the group.

The ACMHR choir combined freedom songs with gospel music to produce a charismatic style of music unique in the civil rights struggle. The use of gospel music was a characteristic of the urban African-American church and Birmingham had a strong gospel music tradition.

Thus, the ACMHR choir's use of gospel music emphasized the ACMHR cultural and religious ties to the African-American community and the indigenous nature of the Birmingham movement.

In the ACMHR mass meetings, singers allowed their emotions to take over, and on many occasions ushers had to restrain them. One choir member remarked that "the choir sings with faith in God, knowing that His power works through their songs and gives them courage to keep singing while struggling for freedom." One of the favorite songs of the choir was "Ninety-nine and a Half Won't Do." Composed by Reese, the song expressed the need for total commitment to the cause. Other songs, such as "God Will Make a Way," expressed absolute faith in God who would give them the power to overcome the pro-segregation forces in the city.[14]

---

[13]Eskew, "ACMHR," 69; Clarke, "These Rights They Seek," 34.

[14]Interview with Carlton Reese, February 13, 1994; Eskew, "ACMHR," 65; Eskew, "But for Birmingham," 196-197.

The ACMHR ushers were formed shortly after the movement began. In Birmingham's churches, ushers provided an opportunity for people to gain a sense of worth and importance. Although a person was a maid or janitor in the secular world, he could put on an usher's uniform or badge and be very visible in church. Most church ushers were females, and this was also true of the ACMHR ushers. Coming from various churches and under the direction of the Reverend Charles Billups, ACMHR ushers met persons at the door, welcomed them into the church sanctuary, kept order, and restrained those who became overly emotional. The ushers saw themselves as providing a service and assisting an organization that was creating change for African Americans in Birmingham.[15]

The influence of the African-American church and its peculiar culture on the ACMHR stands out most vividly in the organization's weekly mass meetings. These meetings were essentially African-American church worship services. The meetings began with a thirty-minute devotional service made up of prayers, spirituals, and meter hymns, followed by singing by the ACMHR choir. The presider, usually ACMHR vice-president, the Reverend Edward Gardner, offered brief remarks. A local supporting pastor delivered a sermon. President Shuttlesworth then made some remarks and the ushers took up the offering. The meetings were very emotional with much shouting. For example, at the meeting of January 23, 1961, the Reverend Oscar Herron, a local pastor, preached. The result was that a dozen women became so emotional that ushers had to remove them from the church. Fellow ministers and ushers had to restrain Reverend Herron from continuing his sermon for fear that the meeting would break into pandemonium or a stampede.

At the meeting of April 17, 1961, in which there was unusual emotional fervor and shouting, Shuttlesworth had to remind the audience that this was not a church but a movement with business to take care of. The emotionalism of the mass meetings, as in an

---

[15]Interview with Fannie Nelson, September 5, 1994; Eskew, "ACMHR," 68.

African-American church, provided not only emotional release but also the courage to fight the forces of segregation in a hostile environment.[16]

Despite ongoing demonstrations and pressure from the ACMHR, only limited gains had been achieved by the ACMHR through 1962. The movement had succeeded in integrating the buses and the train and bus terminals, but schools remained segregated, the city had hired no black police officers, public accommodations were still segregated, and there had been no elevation of black employment. At the urging of the ACMHR, Martin Luther King Jr. made the decision to come to Birmingham. His major reason was to assist the ACMHR achieve its goal of integration in the city.

Two assets that King brought to the Birmingham movement were his national reputation and his ability to attract the national media, assets that observers and scholars have documented well. But King's success in broadening the base of support of the movement and enhancing the church culture that sustained the ACMHR movement were equally significant.[17]

Some segments of the African-American community had not responded to Shuttlesworth's leadership, including pastors of some of the largest churches and leading professionals. King was successful in attracting many of these persons. Some professionals and pastors joined because of their friendship with King. Others because of King's ability to persuade them of the righteousness of the cause.[18]

King's arrival enhanced the religious dimensions of the ACMHR and its church culture. With King's involvement, the ACMHR held meetings every night, instead of just Monday nights.

---

[16]Birmingham Police Report of the ACMHR found in the Southern History Archives of the Birmingham Library for January 23, 1961 and April 17, 1961.

[17]Stephen B. Oates, *Let the Trumpet Sound: The Life of Martin Luther King, Jr.* (New York: Mentor Printing Company, 1985), 202; Eskew, *But for Birmingham*, 296.

[18]Eskew, "ACMHR," 101-105; Interview with John Porter, January 17, 1993.

The meetings were highly spiritual and emotional. Crowds were larger. It was necessary to hold meetings in the larger churches. King, Shuttlesworth, and Ralph Abernathy took center stage. It was at these meetings that persons willing to go to jail came down front after the appeal, just as persons might come down the aisle to join African-American churches after the minister had preached a sermon and asked new believers to join the church.

In addition, King's activities in Birmingham took on religious symbolism. He was arrested on Good Friday, the day of the celebration of Christ's crucifixion. While in jail in Birmingham, he wrote a letter to a group of white clergymen, a letter similar to the prison epistles of Paul.[19]

The climax of the movement in Birmingham began with the decision to intensify the demonstrations using children and Public Safety Commissioner "Bull" Connor's use of dogs and hoses, events that historians of the civil rights movement have well documented. On May 10, 1963, the white business community and the civil rights leaders reached an agreement that called for the integration of public accommodations and the hiring of sales persons and clerks in stores, an agreement that was interpreted by the African-American community as a victory. For many civil rights historians and scholars, Birmingham was the turning point of the civil rights movement that made possible the Civil Rights Act of 1964 and rehabilitated the leadership of Martin Luther King Jr..[20]

---

[19]Adam Fairclough, *To Redeem the Soul of America: The Southern Christian Leadership Conference and Martin Luther Kind, Jr.* (Athens: University of Georgia Press, 1987), 120; Oates, *Let the Trumpet Sound,* 211-222; Malinda Snow, "Martin Luther King's Letter from the Birmingham Jail as Pauline Epistle" in David Garrow, ed., *Martin Luther King, Jr., Civil Rights Leader, Theologian, Orator* (Brooklyn, New York: Carlson Publishing Company, Inc., 1989), 857-873.

[20]The climax of the Birmingham Movement and the agreement reached between the businessmen and the civil rights leaders have been recorded in several books. Among these are Oates, *Let the Trumpet Sound,* 224-233; Ralph David Abernathy, *And the Walls Came Tumbling Down: Ralph Abernathy An Autobiograpy* (New York: Harper & Row Publishers, 1989), 262-269; Fairclough, *To Redeem the Soul of America,* 125-129.

The Birmingham movement showed clearly the importance, power, and central role of the African-American church in the civil rights movement. The church in Birmingham provided the leadership, charisma, funding, and organization for initiating the masses. Fred Shuttlesworth was the acknowledged leader and set the tone, direction, and strategy for the movement. Most of all, the African-American church provided the common religious culture that sustained the movement. Blacks in Birmingham could identify with the church more than the NAACP and other organizations led by middle-class blacks. Martin Luther King Jr. brought to the Birmingham movement a national reputation and the attention of the national mass media, but also equally as important, he helped build a broader base of support for the movement. He also identified with and enhanced the common church culture that made the Birmingham civil rights movement possible.

2

SUSTAINING THE FIGHT:
THE IMPORTANCE OF LOCAL MOVEMENTS

Aldon D. Morris

I am honored to stand in this sacred spot which the world knows as the Sixteenth Street Baptist Church. I thank the pastor of this great church, Christopher Hamlin, for hosting this symposium on the Birmingham movement. I consider it a high point in my academic career to participate on a panel with the Reverends Fred Shuttlesworth and Wyatt T. Walker.

I was born in Tutwiler, Mississippi, in 1949. I knew the Jim Crow system first hand. I drank from colored water fountains, I attended inferior segregated schools. As a six-year-old, I was gripped with fear when Emmett Till was lynched in Mississippi in 1955. I experienced the prison of oppression known as Jim Crow. Reverend Walker and Reverend Shuttlesworth, I want to thank you both personally for being bold captains of a social revolution that toppled Jim Crow. Your dedicated and courageous actions forever changed the life experiences of African Americans. And it changed America as a whole by pushing it towards the kind of democracy promised in the Declaration of Independence and the United States Constitution. I also want to thank the masses of black freedom fighters here in Birmingham and throughout the South who paid the price to overthrow legal racial apartheid in

America. You put into actions Frederick Douglass's dictum that "He who would be free, must himself strike the first blow!"

The Birmingham movement struck a blow heard throughout America and around the world. Let me present my thesis for today. It is this: The Birmingham movement, encompassed within the original organizational framework of the Alabama Christian Movement for Human Rights, and led by the Reverend Fred Shuttlesworth, was the culminating force that shattered the linchpin of the Jim Crow order. If you want to understand how the civil rights movement overthrew racial segregation in America, you must come to grips with the Birmingham movement.

When I first began to study the civil rights movement in the mid-1970s, I was struck by how previous accounts attributed its victory to the Supreme Court, to the actions of the Kennedy and Johnson Administrations, and to the actions of sympathetic northern whites. Dr. Martin Luther King Jr. was given some credit, but he was usually viewed as the charismatic black Moses who single-handedly waved the magic wand that freed his people. But as I delved into the archives and interviewed key participants of this pivotal movement, I developed a different view.

I came to recognize that even though the courts were important, and so were the Kennedy and Johnson administrations as well as sympathetic whites, these were not the critical factors responsible for overthrowing legal segregation. These were secondary factors triggered by deeper, primary factors. And it was these primary factors that dismantled Jim Crow and the oppression which it championed and sustained.

The primary factors were the local movements that were developed following the 1955 Montgomery bus boycott. These local movements had a definite character. First, they were deeply rooted in the black church and usually led by ministers. Second, they were committed to mass nonviolent direct action that directly confronted the forces of racial segregation. Third, they were associated with the charismatic leadership of Dr. Martin Luther King, Jr.

Why was the black church so central to the civil rights movement and its local movements? Wyatt Walker was the first person to make me realize just how important the black church was to the movement. As a young researcher in awe of the movement and its leaders, I walked into Walker's church and began asking him questions about the movement. He gave me a stern look and replied,

> I don't know where the focus is in your study, but just in these first few questions you pose, it seems to me that you are off-center. . . . The key to SCLC as an organization and the key to Martin Luther King's mobilization of a great social revolution in America is not in organizations, it's in the black church. It's in black preachers and black churches.

He continued, "I'm just being very candid with you. I want to make the best use of your time and the best use of my time." I quickly collected myself, and responded, "Reverend Walker, let's talk about the church."

The black church was so crucial to the movement because it was a mass-based indigenous institution respected by black people. Its ministers constituted the bulk of black leadership. The church was largely free of white control and could act independently, if it had the courage to do so. The black church functioned as the repository of black culture that housed and nourished the community's sacred beliefs and cultural expressions, especially black music. The church served as the black community's major communication network. Finally, the church was the community's organizational framework through which important goals could be pursued in a systematic fashion. Because of all these functions, the black church had no rival. It was as E. Franklin Frazier called it, "a nation within a nation."

It follows then, that the black church would become the institutional and cultural backbone of the civil rights movement. The strength and importance of a local movement were determined by the degree to which that community's churches became involved in the movement in terms of providing a mass of people willing to engage in protest, by providing the movement with leadership, finance, and the resolve to face danger and despite the possible consequences.

These local movements were crucial because they became committed to engaging in mass nonviolent direct action. We must remember that Jim Crow was nothing to be played with. Those who dared to violate its rules could expect awful consequences including being fired from jobs, being jailed, being beaten and hung from the limb of a tree. It was a system designed to make people cowards and say "Yessah, boss" to white people who despised them. It was a system that was designed to exploit black people economically and to dominate them politically. It was a system that thrived on keeping black people educationally ignorant and timid. Jim Crow was dedicated to producing meek black people who were afraid to rebel against one of the cruelest systems of oppression ever invented by the human race. And most of the time it achieved its purpose because it was backed up by the guns and laws of Southern states and by terrorist groups such as the Ku Klux Klan.

The job of local movements was to produce a force that could overcome the awesome power of white segregationists. The great achievement of the 1955 Montgomery bus boycott was its revelation that there existed a method of social protest that could boldly confront the Jim Crow system and win. That method was nonviolent direct action. The challenge of spreading that method was monumental. First of all, most blacks, like other Americans, believed in self-defense rather than turning the other cheek when attacked. The demanding task of teaching this new method to the masses was the only solution to this vexing problem, and that required resources and patience.

The most challenging problem of all was to convince people who had been beaten down by centuries of oppression, that they could use the method of direct action to confront their enemy and engage in direct, but unique, combat whose purpose was to overthrow Jim Crow. To be able to generate mass confrontation utilizing nonviolent direct action was the challenge faced by local movements. If local movements failed to meet this challenge, the larger movement was doomed.

As difficult as the tasks were for local movements, they knew that they were not alone. Martin Luther King Jr. and the black masses of Montgomery, Alabama had proven that church-based nonviolent direct action was capable of confronting the Jim Crow system and winning. The people of Montgomery boycotted and sacrificed for over a year. They organized the Montgomery Improvement Association (MIA). They mobilized the churches. They maintained nonviolent direct action in the face of violence and intimidation. Out of that movement came a new eloquent voice that preached nonviolent confrontation and who led by example. The voice was that of the twenty-six-year-old Martin Luther King, Jr. who would become the major American leader of the twentieth century.

In Montgomery, King displayed the ability to commu- nicate the struggle to the nation and the world with an electrifying clarity. He immediately became a charismatic tool that could be utilized by the black community in their quest to overthrow Jim Crow. As James Lawson put it,

> Any time King went to a movement, immediately the focus of the nation was on that community. . . . He had the eyes of the world on where he went and the black community never had that kind of person. . . . It gave the black community an advantage that it never had.

Similarly, Wyatt Walker stated, "Martin Luther King Jr. was a hero, who would go to jail, who would confront redneck racists, speak boldly before them without hating them and taking a club to them, or trying to shoot back. So people imitated . . . King and his cadre. . . ."

In the late 1950s, local movements had to be built from the ground up. It was an arduous task but Montgomery had provided the method and the example by which Jim Crow could be defeated. Equally as important, it thrust up a charismatic black churchman who could not only assist in strengthening local movements, but could link those movements to a national effort to drive the segregationists from the throne of power. But in 1956, it was not at all clear that local communities would seize the day and develop local movements that could elevate the struggle. Birmingham's black community answered the bell.

Before making the claim that Birmingham's local movement was possibly the most significant movement of the entire civil rights movement, I need to provide a larger context. So let me make it clear: Birmingham was not the only Southern city that developed an important local movement. The Reverends Kelly Miller Smith and James Lawson headed one in Nashville. The Reverend C. K. Steele headed one in Tallahassee, Dr. C. O. Simpkins headed one in Shreveport, the Reverend T. J. Jemison headed one in Baton Rouge, the Reverend A. L. Davis headed one in New Orleans and the Reverend Wyatt T. Walker headed one in Petersburg, Virginia. These are but a few. The general point is this: it was these church-based local movements, affiliated with Martin Luther King, that fueled the civil rights movement, making it a powerful social change force.

But what were the factors the made the Birmingham movement extra-special, extra-important? The Birmingham movement stood out because of the character of its leadership, its organizing ability, its dynamic use of nonviolent direct action and its national and international impact.

Fred Shuttlesworth was the unrivaled leader of the Birmingham movement and of the Alabama Christian Movement for Human Rights. A leader sets the tone of a movement. Leadership is responsible for a movement's vision and character. Movement leadership is to be judged by how effectively it attacks the opposition and whether it is able to prevail over that opposition. It is well documented that Birmingham's white power structure developed and maintained one of the most vicious and formidable systems of racial segregation that existed anywhere in the South.

It was headed by Birmingham's Commissioner of Public Safety Eugene "Bull" Connor and backed by state power embedded in the persons of governors John Patterson and George Wallace. It was solidified by the Klan and the White Citizens Council.

Birmingham's racism thrived on black political disenfranchisement, black economic exploitation, and white violence epitomized by the bomb. Birmingham's white power structure controlled the black middle class by throwing a few bones its way in exchange for its docility and its meek leadership of the black masses. By the 1950s, Birmingham's system of racial segregation appeared air tight, ready to endure for centuries. It would take something black and crazy to enter this lion's den and unleash the forces of black liberation.

Fred Shuttlesworth and the black masses who followed him constituted that black and crazy force that stepped boldly into the belly of the beast. All systems of human oppression derive their ultimate power from the fact that those who are oppressed are unwilling to give their life for the sake of freedom. That makes sense because all of us are afraid to die. Fred Shuttlesworth conquered that fear of death. For him, the destruction of racial segregation became more important than his own life. This is why in 1956, when the ACMHR was organized, Shuttlesworth could cry out, "Now, when you organize to fight segregation, that means you can never be still. We gonna wipe it out, or its gonna wipe us out. Somebody may have to die." Shuttlesworth was clear that he himself was ready to die for the cause. He maintained that "I tried to get killed in Birmingham. I tried to widow my wife and my children for God's sake. I believed that scripture which says, "Whosoever will lose his life for my sake shall find it. I had no fear." This was the attitude that was incomprehensible to "Bull" Connor, and to a lot of black people.

A system of oppression cannot endure for long when it is persistently attacked by a leader willing to die for freedom and one who is able to instill that spirit in the hearts of the oppressed. That was the character of Fred Shuttlesworth's leadership.

I wish to make this abundantly clear. A movement is not an individual. Fred Shuttlesworth was successful because with him stood Ruby Shuttlesworth and his children. With him stood Lola Hendricks, Julia Rainge, Georgia Price and Lucinda Robey. With him stood the men who guarded his church and home. With him stood many ordinary people determined to be free. A movement consists of masses of people that organize themselves to do long term battle with oppressors. The Birmingham movement excelled in organizing an oppressed people to overthrow racial segregation. The black church was the central institution through which the Birmingham movement was organized.

The Birmingham Historical Society has produced the evidence which shows that at least sixty black churches hosted movement meetings. From these movement churches came the rank and file participants, the music that galvanized the resolve of the people, much of the money that financed the protest, and the ministerial leadership that guided the movement.

We should take note that organizing the churches was a difficult task, for even though sixty churches participated, at least 400 others did not. What the historical record shows is that the majority of those who did participate were working class churches rather than middle class churches. Those who had the least did the most. But they were enough to provide the great organized force needed to confront segregation.

Now there is a church that has to be singled out. I speak of Bethel Baptist Church, where the movement was headquartered and where Shuttlesworth was the pastor. In terms of movement history, Bethel is a sacred church. The moment that Bethel became the headquarters of the movement, it became the target of the opposition and that is why it was bombed three times and why its members were constantly harassed. Bethel is sacred because much of the strategic and organizational work of the movement occurred behind its stained glass windows. Bethel was to the movement what the White House is to our government. One day, Bethel, you will get your due, and be recognized as a jewel amongst National Landmarks.

Nonviolent direct action came of age in Birmingham, Alabama in 1963. The goal of nonviolent direct action is to create such a massive crisis within an oppressive social order that the authorities of oppression must yield to the demands of the movement before order can be restored. The complete breakdown of social order is achieved through the use of nonviolent tactics by thousands of freedom fighters. In the spring of 1963, the movement's economic boycott froze the business community. Massive demonstrations caused the city to grind to a halt. The jails filled up when over 3,000 people decided that prison cells held more freedom for them than "Bull" Connor's segregated city. And when the going got tough the music of the movement declared that "ninety-nine and a half" would not do.

At this point nonviolent direct action became of age because it paralyzed the effectiveness of high power water hoses, vicious attack dogs, police billy clubs, and the power of the jailhouse. The segregationists had no way out. Indeed, at this point Birmingham's black community had begun to turn the "Bull" into a steer and create the conditions for the concrete walls of segregation to come tumbling down.

The power of the Birmingham movement in 1963 was intensified by the presence of Martin Luther King Jr. and SCLC. Movement geniuses including Wyatt Walker and many others kept that movement mobilized and on track by implementing their enormous knowledge of nonviolent direct action. When King came, the eyes of the nation and the world were fixed upon Birmingham. White segregationists could no longer beat, jail, and kill black people in the dark. They had to do it on the world stage. And they did. But through its disciplined and dignified protests, the movement utilized the violence of the oppressor to educate the world about the injustice of racial inequality. King showed the creativity that could flower behind a locked jail cell when he penned his letter from a Birmingham jail. The Birmingham movement's creative use of nonviolent direct action made clear to the world who were the oppressors and who were the carriers of the democratic torch.

In 1963, the Birmingham movement struck a blow for freedom that was heard throughout the nation and the world. Within the ten weeks following the Birmingham protest, there were at least 758 Birmingham-style demonstrations, with 13,786 people arrested in seventy-five cities in the South alone. The Birmingham movement rocked international relations. The United States was locked into a Cold War with the Soviet Union, each jockeying for super power supremacy. Newly independent third world nations had to make the choice as to whether to join the Communist bloc or to align themselves with democracy and the United States. The Birmingham movement inspired the heads of African nations to ask the U.S. government, "Why should they come into its orbit, given that it allowed black children to be beaten in the streets of Birmingham?" Yes, the Birmingham movement caused an ideological crisis at the highest levels of the American government. The movement was making racial segregation too costly for it to endure.

Because of the domestic and international crises engendered by the Birmingham movement, the White House concluded that it had to act. Attorney General Robert F. Kennedy studied the map of the United States where pins showed trouble spots multiplying daily. He concluded that the federal government could no longer run around the country like firemen putting out brush fires. He told his brother, President John F. Kennedy, that they had to correct the basic injustices. The president responded with a national address in which he explained that, "Now the time has come for this nation to fulfill its promise. The events in Birmingham and elsewhere have so increased the cries for equality that no city or state or legislative body can prudently choose to ignore them."

In his characteristic style, Shuttlesworth kept the pressure on the president when he declared, "Yes, my friends, the new frontier is trying to catch up with the Negro frontier, unless the president moves with dispatch, vigor, and with a degree of dedication, Negroes will be demonstrating in every nook and cranny of the nation—North, East and West." On June 19, 1963,

President Kennedy sent a national civil rights bill to the U. S. Congress, and on July 2, 1964, President Lyndon Johnson signed into law the 1964 Civil Rights bill.

Reverend Shuttlesworth, as a result, you and the black people of Birmingham achieved a major victory because this legislation took the legal teeth out of a segregated regime that had stood for nearly a century. Your seven years of painstaking work had finally paid off. In hindsight, Reverend Shuttlesworth, you and your movement were never crazy. You were sane and the forces of oppression were crazy. You were right when you declared that, "Rattlesnakes don't commit suicide, that ball teams don't strike themselves out. You've got to put them out." Birmingham proved that racists don't transform themselves. You've got to create a force that drives them from the seat of power and the Birmingham movement did just that.

The Birmingham movement was an exemplary movement because of its leadership, its organizing ability, its perfected use of nonviolent direct action and its national and international impact.

But for Birmingham, this nation could still be mired in legal racial segregation. In 1963, the Birmingham movement lifted up the torch of democracy and the world responded. But for Birmingham, the world might never have learned about Fred Shuttlesworth and the great Bethel Baptist Church that head-quartered a great movement for freedom. But for Birmingham, the current government would not have to consider whether Bethel and the fifty-nine other movement churches should be attributed National Landmark status. But for Birmingham, there would be no puzzling discussion as to whether Fred Shuttlesworth is nationally significant, when he and the movement that he led sent shock waves of democracy throughout the nation and the world. Because of Birmingham, now is the time for the government to grant landmark status to Bethel, to Shuttlesworth, and the fifty-nine other movement churches. There is much work still to be done. The struggle continues.

3

"THE CLASSES AND THE MASSES":
FRED SHUTTLESWORTH'S MOVEMENT AND BIRMINGHAM'S BLACK MIDDLE CLASS

Glenn T. Eskew

Former Birmingham Mayor David Vann has called the civil rights district surrounding Sixteenth Street Baptist Church "hallowed ground." Under the Romanesque portals of the brick sanctuary emerged the singing participants of the Children's Crusade in May 1963. At the height of the demonstrations, firemen in Kelly Ingram Park turned their hoses on the Reverend Fred Shuttlesworth, blasting him against the brick foundations of the church and sending him to the hospital at the crucial moment in the biracial negotiations that ended the protest. During the desegregation of local schools in September, a bomb went off in the basement, killing the four youngest victims of the civil rights struggle.[1]

The history of Sixteenth Street Baptist Church reflects the history of black Birmingham. This is the old First Colored Baptist

---

[1]Howell Raines recalled Vann's comment in the *Birmingham News*, November 15, 1992.

Church that under the leadership of the Reverend William Rufus Pettiford followed the accommodationist philosophy of Booker T. Washington and emerged the central church of the black community. Pettiford's ability to work with the white power structure convinced the president of the school board, Samuel Ullman, to build Industrial High School for Negroes that, under Pettiford's protégé, Arthur Harold Parker, became one of the leading black secondary schools in the country. Pettiford convinced the white banker Sigfried Steiner to support the Alabama Penny Savings Company that at one time ranked as the largest black owned bank in America. Pettiford led Birmingham's traditional Negro leadership class by example. Others—most notably A. G. Gaston—followed his method of brokering deals with prominent white men, advocating racial uplift, and accepting segregation over exclusion. Many members of the black middle class joined Sixteenth Street Baptist Church because of Pettiford, and the subsequent ministers who presided here, in particular the Reverends Luke Beard and John H. Cross, rarely strayed from Pettiford's teachings.[2]

As one of the largest African-American meeting places in the city, Sixteenth Street Baptist Church played host to many visiting organizations by renting out the use of its sanctuary. The Southern Christian Leadership Conference used Sixteenth Street Baptist Church in the fall of 1962 for its annual meeting although Reverend Cross complained that the SCLC forgot to pay the electric bill.

---

[2]Wilson Fallin, *The African American Church in Birmingham, Alabama, 1815-1963: A Shelter in the Storm* (New York: Garland Publishing, Inc., 1997), 41, 58-68; on Ullman see Margaret England Armbrester, *Samuel Ullman and 'Youth': The Life, the Legacy* (Tuscaloosa: University of Alabama Press, 1993), 42; on Steiner see Lynne Feldman, *A Sense of Place: Birmingham's Black Middle Class Community, 1890–1930* (Tuscaloosa: University of Alabama Press, 1999); on segregation over exclusion see Howard N. Rabinowitz, *Race Relations in the Urban South, 1865-1890* (New York: Oxford University Press, 1978); on Beard see Nell Irvin Painter, "Hosea Hudson and the Progressive Party," in Merle Black and John Shelton Reed, eds., *Perspectives on the American South, Volume One* (New York: Gordon and Breach, 1981), 121-126.

Nonetheless here is a significant structure intimately linked to the history of the city.

But Sixteenth Street Baptist is not the mother church of the modern civil rights movement in Birmingham. That distinction belongs to Bethel Baptist Church because of the leadership of its pastor, the Reverend Fred Shuttlesworth, and the activist members of its congregation.[3]

Although a native of Montgomery County, Shuttlesworth spent his childhood on Red Mountain. Raised a Methodist, he converted to the Baptist faith and began preaching, first in Selma and then in Birmingham when he answered the call to pastor Bethel Baptist Church in 1953. A year later the United States Supreme Court issued its *Brown* vs. *Board of Education* decision and Shuttlesworth determined to "give [it] my attention." He was ready for action, having rebelled against segregation while working for the military during the war, but Birmingham's traditional Negro leadership class, so accustomed to accommodation, failed to "grasp the significance" of the court's desegregation ruling. Shuttlesworth joined the local chapter of the National Association for the Advancement of Colored People and tried to light a fire under the feet of its old guard officers, but they frustrated his efforts. They elected him membership chairman figuring he would burn up his energy recruiting new dues-payers. Little did they know.[4]

---

[3]Reverend John H. Cross to Reverend G. [sic] W. Gardner, October 29, 1962, Box 33, File 15, Southern Christian Leadership Conference Papers, Martin Luther King, Jr., Center for Nonviolent Social Change, Inc., Archives, Atlanta, Georgia [hereinafter referred to as the King Center].

[4]On Shuttlesworth's background see *Pittsburgh Courier*, February 14, 1959, Fred L. Shuttlesworth Papers, King Center; see also Lewis W. Jones, "Fred L. Shuttlesworth, Indigenous Leader" in David J. Garrow, ed., *Birmingham, Alabama, 1956-1963: The Black Struggle for Civil Rights* (Brooklyn, N.Y.: Carlson Publishing, Inc., 1989), pp. 115-19, 134. The definitive biography of Shuttlesworth is Andrew M. Manis's *A Fire You Can't Put Out: The Civil Rights Life of Birmingham's Reverend Fred Shuttlesworth* (Tuscaloosa: University of Alabama Press, 1999).

In 1955, Shuttlesworth sponsored a petition demanding the City hire black policemen. He asked the Baptist Ministers' Conference to endorse the effort, but its president, the Reverend J. L. Ware, refused, marking the first time this traditional Negro leader opposed the radical activist. Shuttlesworth collected nearly 5,000 signatures and presented the petition to the city commission, but the lynching of Emmett Till cooled any reformist sympathies in city government and the police force remained all white.[5]

Resistance to growing black demands led the state to file an injunction against the NAACP that outlawed the group in Alabama but convinced Shuttlesworth to organize an independent movement. On May 20, 1956, law enforcement officials padlocked the doors to the NAACP office, an act Aldrich Gunn of Bethel Baptist Church recalled set Shuttlesworth off: "That did it. Fred was just not gonna have that." A state of "helplessness and hopelessness" descended upon black Birmingham as demoralized NAACP members wondered what to do.

Early one morning, Shuttlesworth awoke feeling the presence of God and hearing, "They are trying to kill hope, but you can't kill people's hope." The scripture, "You shall know the truth and the truth shall make you free," echoed in his head. Shuttlesworth then knew he was called to lead the movement. He contacted the other activist members in the NAACP and encouraged them to attend a mass meeting on June 5, 1956 to discuss the black community's response to the injunction. Six other pastors, the Reverends N. H. Smith, Jr., T. L. Lane, G. B. Pruitt, R. L. Alford, Edward Gardner, and Herman Stone, joined Shuttlesworth in issuing the call to the public.[6]

---

[5]Lewis W. Jones, "Shuttlesworth," 132-134; the petition, signed by seventy-seven black ministers, is dated July 25, 1955 and is in Box 12, File 43, Albert Boutwell Papers, Birmingham Public Library Department of Archives and Manuscripts, Birmingham, Ala. [Hereinafter referred to as BPLDAM.]

[6]Lewis, "Shuttlesworth," p. 134; *Pittsburgh Courier*, February 14, 1959; Anne Braden, "The History That We Made: Birmingham, 1956-1979," *Southern Exposure* 7:2 (Summer 1979), 48-54; Marjorie L. White, "Research Report," Draft

Birmingham's traditional Negro leadership class opposed the effort. When an older minister told the "hothead" that God said to cancel the mass meeting, Shuttlesworth responded, "Is that so? Now just when did the Lord start sending my messages through you? You go back and tell the Lord that the meeting is on, and the only way I'll call it off is if He comes down here and tells me Himself."[7]

A thousand African Americans showed their support for a new protest movement when they attended the mass meeting on June 5, 1956. Shuttlesworth began: "These are dark days when men would like to kill hope. . . . But hope is not dead. Hope is alive here tonight." Getting to the crux of the matter, he argued: "The Negro citizens of Birmingham are crying for leadership to better their condition. The only thing we are interested in is uniting our people in seeing that the laws of our land are upheld according to the Constitution . . . ." He then acknowledged the risk involved: "The Citizens Councils won't like this. But I don't like a lot of things they do." At that point, Shuttlesworth turned to the Reverend Smith, who announced the "Declaration of Principles" that created the Alabama Christian Movement for Human Rights. The principles outlined the group's Christian and patriotic beliefs while listing its civil rights goals. Smith asked the audience to ratify the resolutions and received a standing ovation.[8]

Several traditional Negro leaders voiced the opposition of the Baptist Ministers Conference to the formation of the Alabama Christian Movement for Human Rights. Shuttlesworth recognized the Reverend Monroe W. Witt, pastor of Kingston's Harmony Street Baptist Church, who expressed his disapproval of the "Declaration of Principles." The Reverend G. W. McMurray,

---

dated August 2, 1977, Birmingham Historical Society, 14-15.

[7]Fred L. Shuttlesworth, "An Account of the Alabama Christian Movement for Human Rights," in Jacquelyne Johnson Clarke, "Goals and Techniques in Three Civil Rights Organizations in Alabama," (Ph.D. dissertation, Ohio State University, 1960), 136-139.

[8]*Birmingham News*, June 6, 1956; *New Orleans Times-Picayne*, June 7, 1956.

pastor of Metropolitan African Methodist Episcopal Church, attacked the effort: "We should think sanely of what we are doing. Birmingham is too over-organized now." Shuttlesworth retorted, "this is not the time for Uncle Toms," and rather than allow the crowd to shout down the opposition, he asked it to vote again for the ACMHR. Twice more the audience roared its approval, then elected Shuttlesworth president of the new organization. Birmingham witnessed the birth of the modern civil rights movement.[9]

While Shuttlesworth had expected opposition from white supremacists, he had not anticipated the out and out rejection he and the ACMHR received from the black middle class. The Reverend Ware led the fight on several fronts: from his position as president of the Baptist Ministers' Association, which represented half of Birmingham's 400 black Baptist churches, from his position as president of the Greater Birmingham Emancipation Proclamation Association, which annually issued paper protests against segregation, and from his pastorate of Trinity Baptist Church in the old black middle class neighborhood of Smithfield. Ware had earned distinction as the city's premier civil rights leader in 1945 when he led returning veterans in a march for the vote, and although he exerted enormous influence within the black community, his activism had long since waned.

Resenting Shuttlesworth's growing popularity, a jealous Ware attempted to destroy the ACMHR, declaring it "too militant for its own good." Shuttlesworth acknowledged the problem as class conflict within the black community: "Many of the upper class persons who worked in the NAACP are professional people who seem to feel that it is almost taboo to align actively with us." Yet he wondered, "Our professional people need to understand that the gap between the class[es] and the masses must be closed. The

---

[9]*Birmingham World*, June 8, 1956, *Birmingham News*, June 6, 1956; Shuttlesworth, "An Account," 136-140.

classes evolved up from the masses and where would you go and what would you do without the masses?"[10]

As members of the masses, Shuttlesworth and the activists in the Alabama Christian Movement for Human Rights set about organizing the black "lower class." Bethel Baptist Church, the headquarters of the movement in Birmingham, sits in the heart of the industrial community of Collegeville located in North Birmingham near iron furnaces and pipe foundries. The congregation of four hundred members of the black working class in 1956 could relate to their minister who had played near the ore mines in Oxmoor and whose stepfather was disabled by silicosis. When the charismatic Shuttlesworth preached of a better day yet to come, they heard him express their goals and aspirations for the future. Others heard him too as the ACMHR linked less than fifty small churches scattered across the industrial district together into Birmingham's expression of the modern civil rights movement.[11]

Respectable working class black people made up the membership of the ACMHR. They were neither of the black bourgeoisie nor of the black underclass. Of the employed members, fifteen percent held skilled or professional jobs such as teachers and preachers, while only a third labored in unskilled positions such as maids and janitors. The rest of the members contributed to the

---

[10]Geraldine Moore, *Behind The Ebony Mask* (Birmingham, Ala.: Southern University Press, 1961), 203; Fallin, *The African American Church in Birmingham*, 133-134; White, "Research Report," 17; *Birmingham World*, June 5, 1956; Jacquelyne Johnson Clarke, *These Rights They Seek: A Comparison of the Goals and Techniques of Local Civil Rights Organizations* (Washington, D.C.: Public Affairs Press, 1962), 66; Shuttlesworth speech before the Fair Share Organization of Gary, Indiana, September 25, 1958, in Box Four, Shuttlesworth Papers.

[11]Marjorie Longenecker White, *The Birmingham District: An Industrial History and Guide* (Birmingham, Ala: Birmingham Historical Society, 1981), 155-56; Lola Hendricks, 1958 Annual Report of the Alabama Christian Movement for Human Rights, "The Movement is Moving," Shuttlesworth Papers; White, "Research Report," 20; for an analysis of the churches in the ACMHR and other information about the local movement see Marjorie L. White, *A Walk To Freedom: The Reverend Fred Shuttlesworth and the Alabama Christian Movement for Human Rights, 1956-1964* (Birmingham: Birmingham Historical Society, 1998).

local economy through semiskilled work, the kind of employment that often reflected the glass ceiling black people hit under segregation. Roughly a thousand people—forty percent male and sixty percent female—belonged to the ACMHR in 1959 according to a survey of the membership conducted by a sociologist. Most were between the ages of thirty and sixty and half owned their own home. They headed small and stable nuclear families. These people saw the forces of destruction then beginning to threaten the black community and they organized the ACMHR in part to strengthen the family. Shuttlesworth preached against "bobtailed and bossy women," drunks, and others who demonstrated "scandalizing Negro morals," as well as those who used guns "as a badge of American manhood." The movement he led reflected the ideology of hardworking Christian black people demanding access to the American Dream.[12]

An intense religious belief that God would end segregation set members of the ACMHR apart from other African Americans in Birmingham. Through weekly mass meetings they expressed this belief by singing gospel music and transcending during the service. The roughly one thousand Baptists and Methodists in the ACMHR in 1959 harnessed a Christian fanaticism that strengthened their organization but alienated the black middle and under classes. Nonetheless, their religious militancy enabled them to stand up to Public Safety Commissioner "Bull" Connor and the Ku Klux Klan.[13]

Unlike its counterparts, the Montgomery Improvement Association [MIA] and the Albany Movement, which as umbrella organizations attracted a wide range of civic groups, the ACMHR stood alone in Birmingham. Before the bus boycott began, Shuttlesworth had met the Reverends Martin Luther King Jr. and

---

[12]Clarke, "Goals and Techniques," 163-173.

[13]Testimonials from ACMHR members reflecting these religious beliefs can be seen in Howard K. Smith, "Who Speaks for Birmingham?" "CBS Reports," May 18, 1961, CBS, transcript in the Tutwiler Collection of Southern History and Literature, Birmingham Public Library.

Ralph David Abernathy, and he attended the organizational mass meeting of the MIA in December 1955. No doubt this experience gave him ideas he applied in Birmingham. Yet the ACMHR was more radical than its contemporaries, for while it combined direct action with the legalistic strategy learned from the NAACP, it never wavered from its dual demands for equal access as consumers and equal access to employment.

The first protest of the ACMHR resulted from the City's rejection of two black applicants for jobs as patrolmen because of the local custom that reserved the better paying jobs to "whites only." Shuttlesworth spoke for the ACMHR when he said, "We feel that if our people have the qualifications then this office should recognize them as applicants for the job." When the Supreme Court ordered the desegregation of Montgomery's buses on December 20, 1956, Shuttlesworth petitioned the Birmingham City Commission to repeal the City's segregated seating ordinance and to hire black bus drivers. Anticipating a no vote at the meeting on the 26th, Shuttlesworth planned to "ride the buses in a desegregated fashion anyway." On Christmas night, white vigilantes answered Shuttlesworth's challenge by tossing six sticks of dynamite at his house.[14]

The bomb landed between the parsonage and Bethel Baptist Church, and while the explosion did extensive damage to both structures, miraculously it did not kill anyone. The blast demolished the house as it blew out the foundations and knocked down the roof. A huge hole appeared in the basement wall of Bethel Baptist Church and the stained glass windows shattered as the brick structure rolled with the explosion. Neighbors ran to the scene and pulled Ruby Shuttlesworth and the children out of the rubble. When the police arrived, several black men harassed them

---

[14]Shuttlesworth, "An Account," 146-49; *Birmingham News*, July 10, August 20, 22, 27, December 20, 21, 26, 1956; *Birmingham World*, July 26, August 1, December 26, 29, 1956; Fred L. Shuttlesworth to City Commission, July 16, 26, 1956, and "Statement of the City Commission," July 10, 1956, Box 24, File 33, James W. Morgan Papers, BPLDAM.

but the appearance of Shuttlesworth restrained their anger. "The Lord has protected me, I'm not injured," he told the crowd of five hundred onlookers. Someone called out, "God saved the Reverend to lead the movement." The next morning when Shuttlesworth spoke to the two hundred ACMHR members gathered to protest Jim Crow, he reflected: "One reason I was sure that God wanted them unsegregated is because I came through this alive. That bomb had my name on it but God erased it off." He then marched his followers outside and boarded the buses. Years later, he explained, "We say we're going to ride and we ride. We do what we say for a change."[15]

The ACMHR's use of direct action set it apart from other black protest groups in Birmingham. In March 1957, Fred and Ruby Shuttlesworth tested the desegregation of interstate travel by boarding a train for Atlanta as a mob of angry klansmen milled about Terminal Station. When the Shuttlesworths attempted to register their children at all-white Phillips High School, vigilantes attacked them. Had Shuttlesworth not heard God's voice tell him, "You can't die here. Get up. I got a job for you to do," he might have been murdered. In contrast to the direct action protests of the ACMHR which attracted violence, the traditional Negro leadership class organized nonthreatening voter registration drives. Having failed to kill Shuttlesworth, vigilantes struck again at his church. A waitress returning home early in the morning on June 28, 1958 saw a fire burning by Bethel Baptist Church and notified the volunteer night watchman, sixty-two-year-old Will Hall. He discovering a paint can packed with dynamite, picked up the bomb and ran it down to the street where seconds later it exploded, sending out shock waves that broke Bethel's replacement stained glass and cracked the plaster ceiling of the sanctuary. Klansmen bombed Bethel Baptist Church a third time on December 14,

---

[15]*Birmingham News*, December 26, 1956; *Birmingham World*, December 26, 29, 1956; *Christian Science Monitor*, December 27, 1956

1962 yet again the congregation repaired the damage and persevered.[16]

Continued segregation on the city buses led the ACMHR to mount a second challenge on October 20, 1958. Announcing that Birmingham's black people would "henceforth ride in any seat available with the dignity which becomes American citizens, " the ACMHR members again boarded the buses. Police arrested fourteen people including Shuttlesworth and held them incommunicado. When three ministers from Montgomery arrived in Birmingham to assist the protest and police arrested them as vagrants, even the Reverend Ware voiced his outrage, and the black community mounted a bus boycott that lasted a month. Yet only when the federal courts ruled in favor of the ACMHR's appealed convictions did Birmingham's transit system desegregate. It took ACMHR direct action and legal appeal to integrate the airport and the city parks. The black college students who planned sit-ins in March 1960 consulted Shuttlesworth for advice. Officers arrested the youth and then picked up the minister, for as the leader of the ACMHR, Shuttlesworth represented the modern civil rights movement in Birmingham.[17]

The Congress of Racial Equality contacted Shuttlesworth and asked the ACMHR to host it on the Birmingham leg of the Freedom Ride. Black and white CORE members intended to test the integration of interstate travel in the Deep South by riding buses from Washington, D.C. to New Orleans. White vigilantes altered those plans when they attacked the buses in Anniston, actually forcing the Greyhound off the highway and boarding the

---

[16]*Birmingham World*, March 9, 1957, *Birmingham Mirror*, March 6, 9, 1957; *Birmingham News*, September 9, 1957; *Christian Science Monitor*, September 10, 1957; the bombing probably resulted from the ACMHR having joined other black groups in asking the city commission to call for a federal investigation of the unsolved bombings. See Box 12, File 43, Boutwell Papers; *Birmingham News*, June 30, July 1, 1958, and for a retrospective, April 8, 1988.

[17]*Birmingham News*, October 14, 17, 20-28, 1958, March 1, 13, April 1, 20, 1960; *Montgomery Advertiser*, October 21, 22, 24, 28, 29, 1958; *New York Times*, April 12, May 4, 1960.

Trailways for the rest of the journey. Notified of the violence, Shuttlesworth dispatched ACMHR volunteers to rescue the stranded integrationists and he warned the police of the approaching bus. Unknown to him was the prior agreement worked out by "Bull" Connor that allowed the Klan to savagely beat the integrationists when they disembarked in Birmingham. Again ACMHR volunteers collected the brutalized CORE members. One white man, James Peck, required fifty-three stitches to his head and, like the Good Samaritan, Shuttlesworth picked Peck up from the hospital and nursed him that night in his own bed. The next morning the integrationists reassembled at Shuttlesworth's house and the ACMHR members helped them catch a plane to New Orleans. Yet activists from the Student Nonviolent Coordinating Committee had decided to continue the Freedom Ride, so they notified Shuttlesworth of their pending arrival in Birmingham and asked for assistance. Again ACMHR played host as local people, the students, and the federal government worked out an agreement that enabled SNCC to catch a bus to Montgomery. Indeed, when the story of the Freedom Ride is retold, the crucial role played by Shuttlesworth and the ACMHR is often left out. This man and the members of this organization and their churches have never received their fair share of the credit.[18]

Yet people in the movement knew of Shuttlesworth and the track record of the ACMHR. When King and the SCLC needed to recoup ground lost during the Albany Campaign of 1962, they brought the national movement to Birmingham. As corresponding secretary of the SCLC and as the president of that umbrella organization's strongest affiliate, Shuttlesworth had encouraged King to combine SCLC with the ACMHR in demonstrations designed to force the city to desegregate public accommodations and to end racial preferences in hiring. On April 3, 1963, the joint campaign began with sit-ins at area lunch counters to emphasize a black boycott of downtown merchants. A week later, Shut-

---

[18]Police Surveillance Reports, May 11, 16, 24, 1961, Folder 9-24, T. Eugene "Bull" Connor Papers, BPLDAM; Smith, "Who Speaks For Birmingham?"

tlesworth led the first protest march. Had it not been for the dedicated members of the ACMHR with their weekly Monday night mass meetings in movement churches such as Bethel, New Pilgrim, and St. James Baptist, St. John AME and Thirgood CME, there would have been no movement at all. Indeed, the "movement was moving," but the involvement of King and the SCLC was not enough to galvanize black Birmingham behind the campaign as the demonstrations sputtered along.[19]

Upon his arrival in Birmingham, King confronted the opposition from the city's traditional Negro leadership class that had plagued Shuttlesworth since 1956. King had expected to see Ware with the ACMHR, and when he learned of the problems he traveled to a meeting of the Baptist Ministers Conference to ask for its blessing. Abernathy recalled that when he, King, and Shuttlesworth entered the room, they interrupted Ware midsentence, received "no burst of applause and no ripple of friendly smiles," and—after King had explained the purpose of the demonstrations—no endorsement.[20]

To compete with Shuttlesworth, Ware had created his own protest groups. In 1956, he formed the Jefferson County Betterment Association but it collapsed when the ACMHR refused to merge with it during the bus boycott of 1958. In response to the student sit-ins, Ware set up the Inter-Citizens Committee in 1960 to shift the focus away from direct action. With the assistance of the Reverend C. Herbert Oliver, Ware documented racial brutality in Birmingham for the United States Civil Rights Commission. In April 1963, Ware marshaled the forces of the traditional Negro leadership class against the ACMHR-SCLC campaign. A week after

---

[19]For an analysis of the events leading up to and including the actual campaign see Glenn T. Eskew, *But For Birmingham: The Local and National Movements in the Civil Rights Struggle* (Chapel Hill: University of North Carolina Press, 1997); Shuttlesworth relied on the secondary leadership of the Reverends Charles Billups, Edward W. Gardner, J. S. Phifer, N. H. Smith, Abraham and Calvin Woods, and also W. E. Shortridge, Lola Hendricks, and Lucinda Robey.

[20]Ralph David Abernathy, *And The Walls Came Tumbling Down: An Autobiography* (New York: Harper and Row, 1989), 238-239.

his first appearance before the ministerial association, King returned to plead the case of the modern civil rights movement. This time he had his friend, the Reverend John Cross, propose a resolution endorsing the demonstrations. Previously Cross opposed the ACMHR but King convinced him to allow SCLC to use Sixteenth Street Baptist Church as a meeting site. Ware refused to recognize the motion. Later he explained, "We are against segregation in all phases, but we haven't taken a specific stand as such. . . . There is quite a bit of dissension, but we would not do anything to handicap the Movement."[21]

Other traditional Negro leaders resisted the ACMHR-SCLC campaign. *The New York Times* reported that "many prominent members of the Birmingham Negro community are known to have opposed a direct action campaign at this time." A. G. Gaston had never supported the local movement and when King arrived, he reluctantly leased rooms in his motel to the group but refused to allow it to use the auditorium in his "ultramodern" building. Emory Jackson, the editor of the black newspaper the *Birmingham World,* privately described Shuttlesworth as an "upside downer" who staged negative direct action "flash dances" that sensationalized civil rights. Jackson favored Ware for his quiet and "constructive" voter registration drives. In public Jackson said little about Shuttlesworth or King as attested by the lack of coverage in the *World*, but he publicly praised Ware for his "responsible leadership." At the end of April 1963—a month into the ACMHR-SCLC campaign—Jackson featured in the *World* a gathering of Birmingham's traditional Negro leaders in Metropolitan AME Church where its pastor, the Reverend G. W. McMurray—who had criticized Shuttlesworth in 1956—recognized Ware for his

---

[21]*Birmingham World*, April 13, 17, 20, 1963; David L. Lewis, *King: A Critical Biography* (New York: Praeger Publishers, 1970), 179.

many contributions. This counter-movement competed with the ACMHR-SCLC.[22]

In an attempt to unify the black masses behind the movement, the ACMHR-SCLC exploited the opposition from Birmingham's traditional Negro leaders. At a mass meeting in the First Baptist Church of Ensley on April 8, 1963, the Reverend Abernathy "scathingly assailed the black 'Bourgeoisie' to the howling delight of the rafter-packed audience" reported a journalist from the *Cleveland Call and Post*. Describing a "roomful of the elite, the Bourgeoisie, the class of Birmingham who are now living on the hill, learning to talk proper," Abernathy ridiculed "their hair tinted various colors, trying to fool somebody. Year before last they lived like us, across the railroad tracks, took baths in a tin tub, and went to an outhouse. Now they are strutting around proper." Suggesting the masses had made the elite rich, Abernathy recommended the audience members "talk with your doctor, your lawyer, your insurance man and withdraw your trade from him if he is not with this movement." As for the black ministers who failed to endorse the campaign, Abernathy recommended "you ought to threaten to cut the preachers' salaries if they don't stand up with you for freedom. They say this is the wrong time and yet they have had 350 years. I want to know when the devil gives the right time." Despite the harsh rhetoric, the ACMHR-SCLC continued to appeal to the black elite for support.[23]

The crisis resulting from the use of school children in May 1963 enabled the traditional Negro leaders to work with the ACMHR-SCLC. King had convinced several friends from Birming-

---

[22]*New York Times*, April 6, 10, 11, 1963; A. G. Gaston, *Green Power: The Successful Way of A. G. Gaston* (Birmingham, Ala.: Southern University Press, 1968), 124-125; the *Cleveland Call and Post*, April 13, 1963, quoted Wyatt T. Walker as saying "Dissention is nothing new. We are just strong enough now, and mature enough, and confident enough, so that we don't mind the white man knowing about our differences." On Jackson see the *Birmingham World*, April 20, 24, 27, 1963; Emory O. Jackson to Anne G. Rutledge, April 5, 12, 1963, Emory O. Jackson Papers, BPLDAM.

[23]*Cleveland Call and Post*, April 13, 1963.

ham's black middle class to join the movement's negotiating team. When the images of firemen training their hoses on nonviolent black youth appeared in the papers, the Kennedy Administration sent an envoy to Birmingham to broker a deal. Because the traditional Negro leaders were eager to get King out of town, they quickly agreed to a truce that fell far short of the local movement's goals. When Shuttlesworth heard of their compromise, he confronted King, an act that made the movement temporarily hold its ground. Nonetheless, by participating in the negotiations, the traditional Negro leaders gained white recognition that legitimated their claim to represent the black community. As Andy Young later recalled, "The leadership fell right back into the hands of the middle class, and had they not been involved at all through the process, they wouldn't have been prepared to bring leadership in the period of reconciliation that followed."[24]

Yet the civil rights demonstrations had spread beyond Birmingham as the oppression there ignited protests in hundreds of cities and awoke the country to a crisis in race relations. It had been a long and difficult struggle, but the local movement begun by the black working class in 1956 finally forced the president of the United States to propose legislation to resolve the crisis in race relations. Passed as the 1964 Civil Rights Act, the legislation reformed the system so that all people could gain equal access to the American Dream. The Reverend Fred L. Shuttlesworth is the man most responsible for that success, but his congregation at

---

[24]Eskew, *But For Birmingham*, 259-297; Andrew J. Young, "And Birmingham" *Drum Major* 1:1 (Winter 1971), 23.

Bethel Baptist and the other unsung ACMHR leaders and volunteers share in that glory.[25]

---

[25]Robert Kennedy later explained "what aroused people generally in the country and aroused the press was the Birmingham riots in May of 1963," John Barlow Martin interview with Robert F. Kennedy, March 1, 1964, John F. Kennedy Presidential Library, Boston, Mass. In response to the 700 demonstrations across America spawned by the campaign, President John F. Kennedy announced on June 11, 1963 that "the events in Birmingham and elsewhere have so increased the cries for equality that no city or state or legislative body can prudently choose to ignore them." A week later the president proposed the legislation that Congress passed as the Civil Rights Act of 1964. See Peter B. Levy, *Let Freedom Ring: A Documentary History of the Modern Civil Rights Movement* (New York: Praeger Press, 1992), 117-119.

4

A Fire You Can't Put Out:
The Meanings of Fred Shuttlesworth and His Movement

Andrew M. Manis

Emanating from the Sixteenth Street Baptist Church in the spring of 1963, as one police officer told it, Fred Shuttlesworth and the civil rights movement had "the whole damn town rocking."[1] Eventually, the movement moved not just this one city, but all of America. Some years later, a former mayor of Birmingham summed up the significance of those events like this: "[T]hose sidewalks on Sixth Avenue running from Sixteenth Street Baptist Church toward City Hall are as sacred . . . as the ground at Valley Forge or Yorktown."[2]

---

[1]Police Report, R. S. Whitehouse, R. A. Watkins to Jamie Moore, April 17, 1963, Eugene T. Connor Papers Box 13, Folder 4, Birmingham Public Library, Department of Archives.

[2]David J. Vann, "The Change From Commission to Mayor-Council Government and the Racial Desegregation Agreements in Birmingham, Alabama, 1961-1963," Paper presented to the Center for Urban Affairs, University of Alabama at Birmingham, November 1977 [revised, 1988], 41.

If Valley Forge and the first American Revolution gave us a hallowed collection of heroes, so during America's Second Revolution did this and other sacred spaces across Birmingham give the nation a group of defiant and relatively unsung heroes. Like the heroes who *are* sung in the biblical Book of Daniel, these were heroes who braved "Bull" Connor's fiery furnace, faced down the powers that were, and replied to Jim Crow: "We'd rather obey God than human beings. We cannot—so help us God—do otherwise." More common than Shadrach, Meshach, and Abednego, they had names like Charles Billups and J. S. Phifer, Ed Gardner and N. H. Smith Jr., Abraham and Calvin Woods. Names like Lucinda Robey, Lola Hendricks, and Georgia Price.

Birmingham's Revolutionaries—all of them members of the Alabama Christian Movement for Human Rights, an organization conceived in defiant response to an Alabama court's injunction outlawing the NAACP. All of them followers of the Reverend Fred Shuttlesworth.[3] For seven years the Alabama Christian Movement confronted Connor and Jim Crow until in 1963, by Shuttlesworth's invitation, Martin Luther King Jr. and the Southern Christian Leadership Conference came to build on what had begun in Birmingham. The hundreds who went to jail that spring were the widened circle that began with the defiant revolutionaries who were inspired by the combative courage, and to them the divine deliverance, of Fred Shuttlesworth.

In describing their transition from slavery to freedom, African Americans have almost always used the biblical language of deliverance. Sometimes it has been the language of Daniel and even more often the language of the Exodus. But always they have sounded the themes of deliverance and liberation. "Go down, Moses," sang the slave spiritual, "Tell ol' Pharoah, 'Let my people go.' " For centuries the Jewish children of that first Exodus have gathered in their homes to commemorate that liberation in the

---

[3]This essay is a distillation of my larger biography, *A Fire You Can't Put Out: The Civil Rights Life of Birmingham's Reverend Fred Shuttlesworth* (Tuscaloosa: University of Alabama Press, 1999).

Passover Seder. For centuries they have re-enacted that sacred event with several ritual questions that amount to "Father, what mean these things?" In like manner the Sixteenth Street Baptist Church, and even more so, Bethel Baptist Church on 29th Avenue North and the other churches were sacred places where another Exodus was preached and prayed for. And the children of that second Exodus, hearing of what happened here, similarly ask, "What mean these things?"

The meanings of Fred Shuttlesworth and the local movement he led are manifold. Most important for the Birmingham movement's national implications was Shuttlesworth's indispensable role in a campaign that was a crucial success for the civil rights movement. Few episodes of the black freedom struggle are as etched into America's collective memory as the images of the police dogs and fire hoses of the 1963 Birmingham demonstrations. The televising of those dramatic events convinced President Kennedy, the Congress, and millions of Americans that civil rights legislation should and could be passed.

In January 1963, Kennedy shied away from introducing such a civil rights bill because he believed Congress was unlikely to approve it. The Birmingham campaign, however, convinced the reluctant president to reorder his domestic priorities to include strong legislation on civil rights. Robert Kennedy later noted that his brother saw the Civil Rights Bill as politically viable only *after* Birmingham. Wyatt T. Walker, then Executive Director of SCLC, insisted that it was the demonstrations that made the critical difference, Calling those events "a major watershed in the history of the Negro in America," Walker pointed out Kennedy's change of strategy between January and June: "In six months, the plight of Negroes had not changed substantively. But," he added, "there *had* been a Birmingham."[4]

---

[4]On the success of the Birmingham demonstrations, see John Walton Cotman, *Birmingham, JFK, and the Civil Rights Act of 1963* [sic]: *Implications for Elite Theory* (New York: Peter Lang, 1989); Glenn T. Eskew, *But for Birmingham: The Local and National Movements in the Civil Rights Struggle* (Chapel Hill: University of

Other elements obviously entered into the *passage* of the Civil Rights Act of 1964, most notably the nation's response to the assassination of President Kennedy and the legislative arm-twisting of Lyndon Johnson, but Kennedy's introduction of the civil rights bill was just as clearly owing to the protests of Birmingham's revolutionaries.

Shuttlesworth and his organization were indispensable to winning that battle, certainly as crucial as the forces who came to the city from Atlanta and the SCLC. While journalistic references at the time ordinarily designated King as the leader of the demonstrations, the activities of the SCLC built on the foundation laid by Shuttlesworth and the ACMHR. Though sometimes viewed as an outgrowth of King's work with the Montgomery Improvement Association, in reality Shuttlesworth's organization was of independent origin and his civic work in Birmingham as pastor of the Bethel Baptist Church predated King's arrival in Montgomery. Then, beginning in 1956, Shuttlesworth and the organization that was in essence the extension of his fiery persona provided consistent agitation and repeated confrontation to the Magic City's Jim Crow system up to and beyond the 1963 protests.

Between the Montgomery boycott and the Birmingham campaign, Shuttlesworth was clearly the most dynamic local leader affiliated with SCLC and at least as early as 1959, he began to lobby King and SCLC to join forces with his ACMHR. That year,

---

North Carolina Press, 1997; Adam Fairclough, *To Redeem the Soul of America: The Southern Christian Leadership Conference and Martin Luther King, Jr.* (Athens: University of Georgia Press, 1987), 134-136. On Birmingham's impact on Kennedy, see Harold W. Chase and Allen H. Lerman, eds. *Kennedy and the Press: The News Conferences* (New York, 1965), 449- 450; Martin Luther King, Jr., interview with Berl I. Bernhard, March 9, 1964, Atlanta, Georgia, Oral History Program, John F. Kennedy Library, 17-18; Robert F. Kennedy in an interview with Anthony Lewis, *Robert Kennedy: In His Own Words: The Unpublished Recollections of the Kennedy Years* (New York: Bantam Books, 1988), 149; Wyatt T. Walker, "The Meaning of Birmingham," *News Illustrated* 1 (May 1964), 1-2; Claude Sitton, Interview with Jack Bass, 1974, Southern Oral History Program, Manuscripts Department, University of North Carolina, Chapel Hill, 11.

in conjunction with Southern Conference Education Fund, the ACMHR published a pamphlet whose title depicted the Birmingham revolutionaries as the vanguard of the civil rights movement—*They Strike Segregation at Its Core!* The pamphlet reviewed Shuttlesworth's activities since 1956 and solicited outside financial support. The entreaty was based on Shuttlesworth's view that as went the struggle in Birmingham, so would go its success throughout the South. "Wherever you live," the tract explained,

> if you believe in human dignity and brotherhood, Birmingham Negroes are fighting your battle. Birmingham is the strongest bastion of segregation in America. When equality and right win there, the key line of segregationist defense will be breached. From then on, victory for human rights will be easier everywhere. Birmingham in a sense is the test for America's future."

SCLC quickly came to share that view.[5]

In April 1959, Shuttlesworth was insisting on more action by SCLC, writing King to complain that he was not attacking segregation in Alabama vigorously enough. He saw civil rights leadership in Alabama as "much less dynamic and imaginative than it ought to be." "When the flowery speeches have been made," he wrote, "we still have the hard job of getting down and helping people. . . . [W]e [SCLC] must move now, or else [be] hard put in the not too distant future, to justify our existence." Looking forward to a forthcoming SCLC board meeting, he hoped that "we can really lay some positive plans for action. . . . Now is the time for serious thinking and practical resulting actions." In June, Shuttlesworth wrote another impatient letter to King reiterating

---

[5]Alabama Christian Movement for Human Rights, *They Challenge Segregation At Its Core!* (Birmingham: Southern Conference Education Fund, 1959), copy in Shuttlesworth Papers, Box 1, Folder 18; Adam Fairclough, *To Redeem the Soul of America: The Southern Christian Leadership Conference and Martin Luther King, Jr.* (Athens: University of Georgia Press, 1987), 58.

his call for action. "I had certainly expected to hear from you further on this matter before this time. . . It is my feeling that the times are far too critical for us to get good solid ideas on what should be done in certain situations, and then take too long a time to put these ideas into action."[6]

In 1960 Shuttlesworth observed student sit-ins in High Point, North Carolina, and convinced King to endorse the tactic. In 1961 Shuttlesworth was the primary contact person in Alabama for the Freedom Rides. He sent some of his followers to retrieve them when one bus was burned in Anniston. When the other busload was beaten in Birmingham, Shuttlesworth's family and church members bandaged their wounds and housed them.

In 1962 Shuttlesworth and Charles Billups were jailed for activities related to the Freedom Rides, remaining incarcerated for thirty-six days. In the fall of that year, Shuttlesworth called on King to hold the annual SCLC Convention in Birmingham and to threaten massive demonstrations. With that threat, merchants removed segregation signs from downtown department stores—but only temporarily. The return of those signs set the stage for Project C (Confrontation) in the spring of 1963.

King thus decided to go to Birmingham because of Shuttlesworth's direct invitation, indeed because of his repeated insistence, and because of a nucleus of available demonstrators Shuttlesworth had developed over the previous seven years. Wyatt T. Walker argued the point forcefully:

> I'm absolutely convinced without any reservation, Birming-
> ham never would have been without a Fred Shuttlesworth.
> You could not have come to Birmingham if there hadn't
> been a Fred Shuttlesworth there. He was not just a preach-

---

[6]Letter, Shuttlesworth to King, April 24, 1959, in Martin Luther King, Jr. Papers, Boston University, Box & 9, cited in David J. Garrow, *Bearing the Cross: Martin Luther King, Jr., and the Southern Christian Leadership Conference* (New York: William Morrow and Company, Inc, 1986), 116; Shuttlesworth to King, June 15, 1959, Martin Luther King, Jr. Papers, Box 9.

er in Birmingham with some people who were interested in human rights. It was the very nature of his persona—his doggedness, his tenacity, his courage, his craziness. I mean all of that congealed to make Birmingham fertile for what we needed to do.[7]

Thus, Shuttlesworth laid the groundwork for and made possible the 1963 demonstrations, which in turn yielded introduction of what eventually became the 1964 Civil Rights Act, federal legislation ending segregation in public accommodations in America. Those demonstrations also laid the groundwork for Selma, which in turn made possible the 1965 Voting Rights Act.

These facts undeniably underscore the national significance of Birmingham's revolutionaries. There are other meanings as well. Accurately to describe Shuttlesworth and his movement requires speaking of their purity or their undiluted character in three important areas.

UNDILUTED BLACKNESS

First, what began in the parsonage of the Bethel Baptist Church and spread to many other churches and eventually to this place where four young martyrs died showed the undiluted blackness of the Birmingham movement and its leader. It has been in scholarly vogue over the past fifteen or twenty years to emphasize the black or African-American roots of the civil rights movement and to de-emphasize white contributions to the movement. For the most part this historiographical emphasis has been right and proper. Many early scholars have sought to note the role of Gandhian nonviolence, but as one black preacher argued that "when Martin marched, they weren't singing no Indian songs. They were singing black spirituals and it was out of that context

---

[7]Interview with James T. Montgomery, M.D., August 4, 1989, 31-32; Interview with Joseph E. Lowery, July 29, 1991; Interview with J. L. Chestnut, December 27, 1989, 11; Interview with Wyatt T. Walker, April 20, 1989, 8.

that he preached."[8] Clearly, the African-American is the most important context for understanding the civil rights movement.

Nevertheless, one cannot deny the contributions of non-blacks to his movement. King *was* educated in a white seminary and graduate school. He readily acknowledged his intellectual debts to Gandhi, Reinhold Niebuhr, Walter Rauschenbusch, Paul Tillich, Edgar S. Brightman, as well as to African-American mentors like Benjamin Mays and Howard Thurman. In addition, a number of whites were active participants in the SCLC as advisors and aides to King, among them Stanley Levison, Harry Wachtel, Harry Boyte, and Glenn Smiley.[9]

In contrast to King, however, Shuttlesworth emerged from a relatively impoverished southern, rural, working class family. From Cedar Grove Bible Academy in Mobile to Selma University to Alabama State College, *all* of Fred Shuttlesworth's education was in black institutions. Not an avid reader of white theologians or preachers, Fred Shuttlesworth had no white models or mentors. His influences were the black church, first the African Methodist Episcopal Church and eventually the Baptist tradition, but from beginning to end, undiluted by any white perspective or, as some would say, white *tampering*. Nor did Shuttlesworth have any significant white participants or advisors in the ACMHR. In this way, Shuttlesworth better exemplified the poorer backgrounds of most southern blacks in the civil rights era. This helps explain the long-lasting loyalty Shuttlesworth won from his followers in Birmingham. While some pastors and laypersons in the middle-class black churches disliked his "demonstrate now, work out the details later" style, his charisma and confrontational personality attracted working class blacks in large numbers. Jonathan MacPherson, an activist professor at Birmingham's Miles College thus argued that Shuttlesworth's followers "just loved the man,

---

[8]W. J. Hodge, interview with author, April 2, 1984.
[9]See Fairclough, *To Redeem the Soul of America*, 5, 8, 23-25, 176.

because he could articulate the innermost feelings of the rank and file. . . ."[10]

In addition, the respective preaching styles of King and Shuttlesworth suggest a significant difference. Shuttlesworth's homiletical approach originated with the black folk pulpit and did not borrow heavily from white princes of the pulpit such as Harry Emerson Fosdick, George Buttrick, or J. Wallace Hamilton as did King's.[11] He was much less likely than King to write out his sermons, either in outline or in full manuscripts. Perhaps most significantly, I would argue that Shuttlesworth was more likely to engage in what some consider a hallmark of black preaching, the "whoop."

Scholars like James Cone have rightly argued King's preaching was more "black" when he spoke to exclusively black audiences. Still, at least while in seminary King shied away from what he considered the emotionalism of the black church, which he said he didn't understand and which embarrassed him.[12] In fact, Lawrence Edward Carter Sr., dean of the King International Chapel at Morehouse College, has indicated that many African-American ministers saw King as a good "intellectual preacher," but not in the same homiletical league with "whoopers" like National Baptist Convention president J. H. Jackson or Aretha's daddy, the Reverend C. L. Franklin.[13]

---

[10]Interview with Jonathan MacPherson, August 4, 1989, 14, 18.

[11]On King's borrowing from other preachers, black as well as white, see Keith D. Miller, *Voice of Deliverance: The Language of Martin Luther King Jr. and Its Sources* (New York: Free Press, 1992).

[12]King expressed his reaction against the black church in a paper written at Crozer Theological Seminary, "An Autobiography of Religious Development." In a later interview he said: "I had doubts that religion was intellectually respectable. I revolted against the emotionalism of Negro religion, the shouting and the stomping. I didn't understand it and it embarrassed me." See William Peters, "The Man Who Fights Hat With Love," *Redbook* 117 (September 1961): 94.

[13]Lawrence Edward Carter Sr., telephone conversation with author, October 27, 1998. Carter emphasizes the influence of King's mentor and college president Benjamin E. Mays. Carter has studied hundreds of Mays's sermons and holds that though Mays's preaching exhibited the call-and-response cadence characteristic

By contrast, some of Shuttlesworth's early parishioners felt that he ran into conflict at First Baptist Church Selma in part because of his penchant for "country preaching" or "whooping," which a number of his sophisticated middle-class members disliked.[14] For these reasons one may fairly argue that in Fred Shuttlesworth and his followers can be seen the undiluted African-American character of the Birmingham movement.

---

of African-American preaching, he was not a "whooper." See Lawrence Edward Carter Sr., *Walking Integrity: Benjamin Elijah Mays, Mentor to Martin Luther King Jr.* (Macon: Mercer University Press, 1998), 14.

[14]There are many names given to the sermonic genre known as the "whoop." Among these are "moaning," "mourning," "tuning" ("getting a tune"), "zooming," "coming on up at the end," or "the climax." More recently, Henry H. Mitchell, who has written extensively on this form, called it "the celebration." See Mitchell, *Celebration and Experience in Preaching* (Nashville: Abingdon Press, 1990), 12, 61-75; *Black Preaching* (Philadelphia: J. B. Lippincott Company, 1970), 162-177; Albert J. Raboteau, "'A Fire in the Bones': The Afro-American Chanted Sermon," Occasional paper, n.d., copy in author's possession. The term "hacking" for the gasping delivery was used by Louretta Wimberly, interview with the author, September 19 and October 5, 1994, 29. Though uncommon, the expression is not unique to her. On First Baptist Selma's rejection of Shuttlesworth's "country singing" see the author's interview with J. L. Chestnut, December 27, 1989, Selma, Alabama, 24-25. Later, as pastor of Bethel Baptist Church in Birmingham, Shuttlesworth is remembered to have "whooped" almost every Sunday. See interview with James Roberson , August 2, 1989, Birmingham, Alabama, 4, 25-27.

UNDILUTED COURAGE

Though often arousing his supporters at church or mass meetings with the unpolished rhetoric of the black folk pulpit, he primarily appealed to them through daring acts of defiance against his principal antagonist, Commissioner of Public Safety, Eugene "Bull" Connor. His actions inspired the courage and confidence of ordinary blacks who loved and adored him. In blunt, unembellished terms, the raw emotionality of his expression captured their feelings in ways that even King sometimes did not. More importantly, however, his bold confrontations fundamentally embodied the feelings of poor and working class blacks. Longtime friend James Armstrong compared Shuttlesworth to King, noting: "Now Martin knew how to say it; Fred know how to do it. . . . I've had good preachers to preach to me, but Fred has preached to me in action."[15]

In keeping with the biblical theme of deliverance, Shuttlesworth was a Daniel in his own right. He repeatedly put himself in the lions' den, often saying matter of matter-of-factly, "I tried to get killed in Birmingham." So in 1956 he announced that his followers would begin riding buses in a nonsegregated manner on December 26, whether city ordinances were changed or not. Such defiance could not go unanswered by the Klan, so on Christmas night they left a present of fifteen sticks of dynamite under the floor beneath the bed in which he lay. The house and the church next door were greatly damaged, but Shuttlesworth emerged without a scratch. This was the first of three bombings of the Bethel Baptist Church, but his deliverance from this one led him and others to conclude: "That bomb had my name on it, but God erased it off. . . . God saved me to lead the fight." The next day, just as promised, the fight was on and blacks rode in the front of the buses.

---

[15]James Armstrong interview; Interview with Colonel Stone Johnson, July 31, 1991.

The next year Shuttlesworth announced he would be enrolling his daughters in the all-white Phillips High School. A few days before the announced date, Klansmen castrated a young black man named Judge Aaron, passing on the message that the same treatment awaited blacks who tried to integrate the schools. There was little question that Shuttlesworth was the intended recipient of the message. On the day itself, he descended in his own fiery furnace. As he approached the school, his car was met by a mob of 15-20 thugs who beat the preacher with bats, bicycle chains, and brass knuckles. The next day the beating was depicted on page one of the *New York Times*, but in part because the event occurred on the same day as other dramatic events surrounding the desegregation of Little Rock's Central High School, the incident did not receive the national attention it otherwise might have. In the aftermath of the beating, Shuttlesworth the pastor said, "This is the price one pays for freedom." The pastor's wife Ruby, who had been stabbed in the buttock during the melee, said her only regret was that modesty would not permit her to show off her scar at the next mass meeting![16]

After the Freedom Rides left Birmingham for Montgomery, CORE and SCLC leaders planned a special service to honor the Riders at Ralph Abernathy's church. Word of the service emerged in the media, and as dusk approached mobs began to gather around the church. Martin Luther King, the main speaker for the evening, arrived at the airport in late afternoon and was escorted by federal marshals to the church on Ripley Street. James Farmer, Director of CORE, was also scheduled to arrive that afternoon, and was met by Fred Shuttlesworth at the airport. By the time they arrived, the mob around the church exceeded a thousand in number and had begun beating up blacks, closing in on and before long, besieging the church.

"Can you get me into that church, Fred?" Farmer asked uneasily.

---

[16]The *Birmingham News*, September 9, 1957; Author's interview with the Shuttlesworth's physician, James. T. Montgomery, M.D., August 4, 1989.

"Wrong question, Jim. The only question to ask is: How will I get you in?"

As they came within a couple of blocks of the church, a crowd of whites waving Confederate flags and shouting rebel yells blocked the car and began to rock it back and forth. Shuttlesworth slammed the car into reverse, screeched to a stop once out of the mob's grasp, U-turned, and tried another approach. Blocked again, Fred turned and headed for a black taxi stand. "I have Jim Farmer," he told a cabbie, "How can I get him into that church?" The cab driver suggested they try a third route, park the car, walk through a nearby cemetery, and approach the church from the rear. Shuttlesworth obliged, but once they crossed the cemetery, they realized the mob had blocked that way as well.

"Jim, we have no choice, we'll have to go right through them!"

"We're going to have to do *what*?" replied a wide-eyed Farmer.

"We're gon' have to walk through that mob!" he repeated.

Before Farmer could answer, however, Fred began to march into the teeth of the horde, shouting, "Out the way. Let me through. Step aside," and elbowing his way toward the church. Farmer, a much larger man than his trailblazer for the day, scuttled up to follow in Shuttlesworth's train, while the ocean of angry white hoodlums obeyed his word. Like the parting of the Red Sea, a path opened up through an ocean of angry whites, allowing Shuttlesworth and Farmer to make an exodus into the "safety" of First Baptist Church. Less inclined toward seeing the miraculous, Farmer chalked the incident up to what was called "the crazy nigger syndrome—Don't mess with that nigger, he's crazy."[17]

Such actions suggested that what was needed among Birmingham's blacks was a leader who, as one Birmingham minister put it,

---

[17]Shuttlesworth interview, May 29-June 1, 1990; Shuttlesworth interview, March 10, 1984, 24-25; James Farmer, *Lay Bare the Heart*, 204-205; Telephone interview with James Farmer, May 5, 1993; Henry Hampton and Steve Fayer, eds., *Voices of Freedom: An Oral History of the Civil Rights Movement From the 1950s Through the 1980s* (New York: Bantam Books, 1990), 91.

"couldn't lose nothing but his life." Shuttlesworth inspired and galvanized support for the struggle in Birmingham and the South by his almost legendary willingness, even eagerness, to sacrifice his life in reckless defiance of Jim Crow. For this reason Martin Luther King Jr. called him "one of the nation's most courageous freedom fighters," a testimonial echoed by virtually all veterans of the civil rights movement.[18]

Some years ago the film *Glory* told the story of the 54th Massachusetts Infantry, the first colored regiment in the Civil War. The night before their suicidal attack on the Confederate Fort Wagner, the film shows the soldiers in a religious testimony meeting. At a climactic point the character played by Morgan Freeman tells his comrades, "If tomorrow is that great gettin' up mornin', then let's let our loved ones know we went down standing up." Historian Gerald Linderman described the experience of Civil War soldiers as "embattled courage."[19] One need not be a partisan to see in Fred Shuttlesworth an embattled courage in pure, undiluted form. If we Americans patriotically celebrate and mark as sacred the places where such sacrifices were made to defend freedom on foreign shores, it is more than appropriate that we celebrate and mark as sacred the places, like Bethel Baptist Church, bombed three times in a struggle to extend freedom on our own streets.

UNDILUTED AFRICAN-AMERICAN SPIRITUALITY

An incident typifying not only Fred Shuttlesworth's role in Birmingham's civil rights struggles, but in many ways his life and ministry, occurred at a mass meeting one Monday night in 1959.

---

[18]Quotations on Shuttlesworth: Interview with Charles Morgan, May 24, 1989, 34; Ed Gardner, interview in Howell Raines, *My Soul is Rested: Movement Days in the Deep South Remembered* (New York: G. P. Putnam's Sons, 1977), 122; Martin Luther King, Jr. *Why We Can't Wait* (New York: New American Library, 1964), 51-52.

[19]Gerald F. Linderman, *Embattled Courage: The Experience of Combat in the American Civil War* (New York: Free Press, 1989).

For several consecutive weeks the Birmingham Fire Department had served as the city's instrument of harassment and intimidation, regularly interrupting ACMHR mass meetings. On this occasion, again, the wail of sirens drowned out the voices from the pulpit of the St. James Baptist Church. Moments later, firefighters rushed into the church sanctuary wielding hoses and axes, ostensibly searching for a fire. Standing up and interrupting a speech by ACMHR treasurer William E. Shortridge, Shuttlesworth asked the firefighters, "Gentlemen, what are you looking for?" Apprizing Shuttlesworth that he had received a "report" of a fire in the building, the fire chief asked Shuttlesworth to clear the aisle of people.

Suspecting that the real purpose of the fire department's arrival lay in stampeding the meeting, and exasperated by the repeated interruptions, Shuttlesworth agitatedly replied, "Now Chief, we're just tired as hell of "Bull" Connor harassing us and we are about ready to just all of us go to jail. If Bull's got room enough to arrest all the thousands of us, okay. We are just tired! We are not going to move!"

"This is no trick, Reverend," the chief pleaded with the preacher, beginning an explanation of the operative fire codes. Knowing he would eventually be forced to give in, but wishing to encourage his onlooking followers, Shuttlesworth used the situation to fullest advantage. "Chief," he demanded, "can you assure me that this isn't "Bull" Connor harassing us? Because if this is "Bull," we are staying! You will have to drag us out!"

Receiving the chief's promise, the leader ordered the meeting moved to another church a few blocks away. Before leaving the premises, however, Shuttlesworth got in one last zinger: "Y'all think it's a fire in here? You know there ain't no fire here. The kind of fire we have in here, you can't put out with hoses and axes!"[20]

---

[20]Fred L. Shuttlesworth, interview with James Mosby, September, 1968, Cincinnati, Ohio, Ralph Bunche Oral History Collection, Moorland-Spingarn Research Center, Howard University, 26-28; Shuttlesworth interview with Joyce

Perhaps there *was* no fire in St. James Baptist Church that night, but in Fred Shuttlesworth there burned a fire that persisted throughout a lifetime of ministry to African Americans, both in the church and in the streets. As he moved from anonymity as a young pastor to national notoriety as a civil rights leader and finally to status as an icon of the movement, "a fire you can't put out," has burned in him brightly. Theologian James H. Evans Jr. recently wrote of the "heavenly fire" of black Christianity. Similarly, social critic Cornel West drew attention to what he calls a "combative spirituality," by which he means an eager, joyful spirituality that preserves meaning by fighting against claims of inferiority. West says that this combative spirituality is a subversive joy that in the midst of political struggle transforms tears into laughter. "Fiery glad" instead of "fiery mad," this distinctively African-American spirituality looks disappointment and despair and death in the face and declares that beyond all these there is hope. Fred Shuttlesworth embodied in undiluted fashion both these elements— "heavenly fire" and "combative spirituality."

Perhaps more than anyone in the entire civil rights movement, Shuttlesworth incarnated the fiery "combative spirituality" at the heart of African-American religion. The fire hoses of 1963, which never unloaded a drop of water on King or Abernathy, slammed

---

Ladner, November 19, 1969, Cincinnati, Ohio, cassette tape recording, Oral History Program, Martin Luther King, Jr., Center for Nonviolent Social Change; see also transcript of Fred L. Shuttlesworth and Charles Billups v. Eugene T. Connor and Jamie Moore, November, 1960, Fred L. Shuttlesworth Papers, MLKC, 31-32; In a 1964 article, Shuttlesworth wrote: "We have been used to police attending mass meetings since 1958, but they came with sirens screaming, lights flashing, fire axes, rushing into buildings hunting 'fires' which were not there—but failing to stampede Negroes or to extinguish the fire that wouldn't go out." See Fred Shuttlesworth, "Birmingham Shall Be Free Someday," *Freedomways*, 4 (Winter 1964): 10. The incident at St. James Baptist Church took place on December 8, 1959, according to testimony in *Shuttlesworth v. Connor*, November 22, 1960, transcript in Shuttlesworth Papers, Box 3, MLKC.

Shuttlesworth against the side of this church building and bruised his ribs. But they never extinguished "the fire you can't put out."[21]

Shuttlesworth's combustible persona burned hot against those forces he saw as enemies of righteousness and justice, attracting true believers to its flame. His life reveals in very clear form something about the nature of African-American religion. Lit in an impoverished and rural Southern home and fueled in the hearth of the African-American church, Fred Shuttlesworth's fiery and combative spirituality flamed most dramatically in its encounter with Birmingham and "Bull" Connor.

In 1992, Benno Schmidt, the former president of Yale University, made a speech to the National Press Club. In the question and answer period that followed, he made an offhand reference to "Bull" Connor. He could invoke *Connor's* name without feeling the need to identify him, while the name of the drama's chief protagonist has dropped from America's historical consciousness. That may be the best reason of all to attend to his story.

So as I close, if you will indulge the preacher in me, I would say that America still needs to listen to Birmingham's revolutionaries, but also to their ancestors in the slave quarters and the brush arbors. There, in what was called the ring shout, the slaves sang and danced in the Spirit, rhythmically moving in a circular direction—a holy song and dance that bore the marks of their free and African past. Every day the long, sad shadows moving clockwise around the sundial reminded them of their present world of enslavement. But in their ring shout they found the prophetic courage to move *counter-clockwise*, against the movement of the sun, against time as their masters defined it. And in their circle of faith,

---

[21]On the central elements of African-American religion see James H. Evans Jr. *We Have Been Believers: An African-American Systematic Theology* (Minneapolis: Fortress Press, 1992), 2; Cornel West, *Prophetic Fragments* (Grand Rapids: William B. Eerdmans Publishing Company 1988), 6; see West's interview with Bill Moyers in *Bill Moyers, A World of Ideas II: Public Opinions from Private Citizens* (New York: Doubleday, 1990), 105-106. The distinction between "fiery glad" and "fiery mad" is emphasized by Henry H. Mitchell, *Celebration and Experience in Preaching*, 63.

they symbolically sang and danced their resistance to the life of slavery around them.[22]

Today, as we remember Birmingham's heroes, let us also learn something from the ways of their ancestors. Let us follow them, and like Fred Shuttlesworth, dance out that joyful, fiery African-American spirit against the grain of a still-race-conscious culture. Let us also dance against the grain of earlier consensus, focusing primarily on King and the national movement, to give historic credit where it is also due. So circle up. Circle up with Brother Frederick Douglass . . . and line up with Sister Sojourner Truth . . . and fall in behind Fred Shuttlesworth and these Birmingham revolutionaries . . . and get in that circle behind Addie Mae and Carole and Denise and Cynthia—those four little saints blown by hatred from this church into the very arms of God. Circle up with them all. Circle up and emulate their courage and, if you are so inclined, pray for the day when we can sing as truly as did they:

> Slav'ry chain done broke at last—
> Gon' praise God 'til I die!

---

[22]This interpretation of the ring shout is suggested by Sterling Stuckey, *Slave Culture: Nationalist Theory and the Foundations of Black America* (New York: Oxford University Press, 1987), 40.

5

THE HISTORICAL SIGNIFICANCE OF BIRMINGHAM

Wyatt T. Walker

Birmingham, Alabama's claim to fame prior to Martin Luther King's advent on the American scene was two-tiered. It was heralded as the South's largest industrial center and held the dubious distinction of being the South's *biggest and baddest* city in race relations. People of African ancestry were held in a vise-like grip of social and economic deprivation. Prior to 1963, the power structure of the city was a willing partner in maintaining the status quo of segregation forever. Even as the industrial giants of the North began to invest their considerable resources in the development of Birmingham, the mind-set was anti-union, anti-Catholic, and of course, anti-black.

As in other segregated communities across the South, the humanity of people of African ancestry survived (barely) through its internally developed infrastructure of religious life and business enterprises restricted principally to black life. People of color in Birmingham, Alabama entertained little thought of where the mainstream was located and held no hope to be a part of it.

Then, without prior warning of any sort, the Reverend Fred Lee Shuttlesworth became the pastor of the Bethel Baptist Church. Under Shuttlesworth's courageous leadership, Bethel became the germ-center of a human rights struggle that would claim international attention and forever change the landscape of both social and political demographics of the entire South. I am aware that is a large claim but it is verified by any cursory or intensive view of America's Southland *before Birmingham* or *post Birmingham*. The specific reference is to the campaign of 1963 orchestrated jointly by the Alabama Christian Movement for Human Rights and the Southern Christian Leadership Conference. All pundits, informed and uninformed, are in agreement that the Birmingham movement is the chief watershed of the nonviolent movement in the United States. It marked the maturation of SCLC as a national force in the civil rights arena of the land that had been dominated by the older and stodgier NAACP. It catapulted Shuttlesworth into an acceptability and credibility that had eluded him for too long despite his tenacity and courage.

Shuttlesworth's ACMHR was born in the wake of Alabama racists outlawing the NAACP. It became a *voice crying in the wilderness* and Shuttlesworth was its major prophet. Formed in 1957 in the wake of the highly successful Montgomery Bus Protest, SCLC had sputtered organizationally until 1960. Its supportive role in the Congress of Racial Equality's (CORE) Freedom Ride and the Albany campaigns gave promise of what it might become. Birmingham's intransigence to ACMHR's moderate demands provided the *zeitgeist* for a history-making movement. King and Shuttlesworth frequently disagreed on strategy on the southern scene but Birmingham brought them together in a marvelous amalgam of mind and spirit. Sometimes the road was bumpy but the religious mooring of the Movement made the rough places plain.

How was this unpredictable alliance forged? Careful review of the development of the nonviolent movement in the nation will suggest that in some sense a Birmingham, if not predictable, was probable. Nonviolence on a mass scale in race relations made its initial appearance in the most unlikely of places and with an equally unlikely cast of characters.

Montgomery, Alabama, the seat of the old Confederacy, known too for its intransigent racism as well as its seemingly complacent Negro inhabitants, had trudged along in Southern-style apartheid until Vernon Johns became the pastor of the Dexter Avenue Baptist Church, frequented largely by middle class Negroes with an understandable penchant to be persnickety. (The church is located on the major avenue leading to the state of Alabama's Capitol Building.)

Vernon Johns was a pulpit personality of legendary skills with an elephantine memory that greatly served his enormous intellect and combined with an unabashed passion for justice on the race issues of the Deep South. Johns and Dexter met head-on like oil and water. Johns complained openly and loudly that Dexter's stiffness made them hostile to the inclusion of Negro Spirituals in the worship service. His confrontation with Dexter was in counterpoint to his confrontations with the white power structure in Montgomery. His brief tenure was marked by a series of running battles with both the Dexter church and the city of Montgomery, culminating with his resignation/dismissal in the early 1950s.

The high point of Johns's gadfly-like activities on race matters was his indictment for a sermon subject posted on the bulletin board of the Dexter Church. Martin Luther King Jr. said to me, on more than one occasion, that the success of the Montgomery Bus Protest had a direct connection to Johns creating a climate of discontent in the minds and spirits of Montgomery citizens of African ancestry.

Martin Luther King Jr., well-born to deeply religious parents in Atlanta, Georgia, seemed to be the most unlikely player in the unfolding drama of race politics of the Deep South. Superficially, Dexter may have presumed he was made for the petit bourgeoisie of Montgomery's black community. Armed with a Ph. D in Systematic Theology from Boston University, as a promising young theologian with a record academically of great competence, after a reasonable stint as a pastor, he appeared to be on a fast track to succeed Benjamin Mays as president of Morehouse College. His intellectual prowess seemed ideally suited to Dexter's taste. They were relieved that he gave no evidence that he possessed the incendiary spirit and passion of the recently departed Vernon N. Johns.

Then Rosa Parks sat down and black Americans in Montgomery began to stand up. A seamstress and an officer of the local NAACP, Mrs. Parks had a long day and in spite of her being the epitome of gentility, but *that day* her inner spirit cried "Enough!" of this idiocy of segregation. She was sitting in a black seat on the bus. But the driver, as was the custom in Montgomery, insisted she relinquish her seat for a white passenger. Her refusal prompted the predictable arrest and booking that led to the famed Montgomery Bus Protest that ushered in the aforementioned nonviolent mass action in what became a major assault on the institution of segregation in the Deep South.

From the successful 381-day boycott of the buses in Montgomery, all else that followed were children of the encounter that rooted Rosa Parks to her seat. Edward Nixon, a Pullman car porter, played a strategic role. But from slavery to the present, it became the task of the African-American church leadership that laid the foundation for an earth-shaking social revolution that captured the world's attention and cast the shadow of Martin King's leadership across the nation's landscape.

It required several years for the nation, black and white, to digest what had occurred in Montgomery. Pundits of social change in race matters presumed in error that Montgomery was a quirk of history. As the nation turned to other matters, the sit-in movement engulfed the South's variety stores like a prairie fire during a drought. Nearly a hundred cities over the course of the early spring and summer of 1960 endured the assault of thousands of college and high school students emulating the four North Carolina young men who had just read a comic book version of the Montgomery Bus Protest and initiated what became the second development in the nation's nonviolent revolution. It was an exciting and heroic summer with countless arrests, boycotts and physical attacks on the demonstrators that in no way deterred the intensity of the students' purpose. The sit-ins in the South prompted sympathy demonstrations in the North and lunch counter segregation capitulated as had intra-city bus segregation a few years earlier.

Within a year, CORE re-instituted the Freedom Rides. It was a legal paradox that the issue of interstate travel had been judicially settled with the Irene Morgan case of 1947. However, the Interstate Commerce Commission never enforced the court's ruling and citizens of African ancestry suffered the indignity and humiliation of segregated interstate travel for the next fourteen years. Montgomery and the sit-ins became the introduction and first chapter of a new saga in race relations protest. The Freedom Rides became chapter three with a bi-directional attack from east and west that focused on Jackson, Mississippi. Hundreds of Freedom Riders arrived in Jackson to submit to arrest and jail terms in the Hinds County Prison and/or Mississippi's notorious Parchman Prison. The summer-long assault and ensuing trials at Jackson buried segregation in interstate travel forever, and chapter four's venue was Albany, Georgia.

The pecan country of southern Georgia witnessed Albany I and Albany II in the brief course of a year's time. The Student Nonviolent Coordinating Committee (SNCC) joined one of the most powerful movements of the South up to that time. However, a Mexican stand-off resulted after SNCC invited King and SCLC to join the campaign and the consequent intramural squabbling marred the effort. Louis Lomax, an African-American journalist, declared that Martin Luther King Jr. left Albany, Georgia *in his most humiliating defeat.*

It needs to be noted that Lomax never set foot in Albany, Georgia. The forces of segregation were forced into some telling concessions: the parks were closed as were the libraries and bus station facilities. The crushing boycott bankrupted the local bus company. The invaluable lesson gained for the movement was the important experience of learning how to mobilize an entire community to assault segregation. On the downside, the media heralded segregationist police Chief Laurie Pritchett as muting the nonviolent campaign with his counter-tactic of nonviolence which was nothing more than non-brutality. The media bought the hypocrisy, hook, line and sinker, without the appropriate discernment that nonviolence is only operative in a moral environment and segregation has always been immoral. Dr. King, smarting under the impasse in Albany determined that if nonviolence was to be proven valid, then SCLC had to take on the biggest and baddest city in the South, Birmingham, Alabama! The plan of Birmingham, "Project C" (for "confrontation") is now legend and Birmingham became the most important chapter of all.

Some chroniclers of the Birmingham era infer that the King/Shuttlesworth alliance was an uneasy one; not so! Its value was that the alliance was dynamic. These two activist giants nourished each other with their respective strengths and weaknesses. Birmingham could never have become what it was without Martin Luther King Jr. and Fred Lee Shuttlesworth. The two organizations complemented each other; the solid-rock character of the ACMHR on the local scene provided the endurance for a such a campaign and SCLC's professional staff, some with considerable skills and experience, provided the know-how to keep the nation's and the world's attention fixed on Birmingham. Together, they produced a fire that water could not put out!

On the last day of January 1963, I began a series of visits to the Magic City in preparation for laying the groundwork for what became "Project C." In a two-day retreat at the Dorchester Center in southeastern Georgia, in early December of 1962, ten or twelve of Dr. King's closest confidants assembled to consider the draft I had prepared for Project C.

My understanding of Dr. King's intent to make Birmingham the venue for the next major nonviolent assault on segregation would require the Movement to confront the demonic forces of segregation and discrimination. My working paper was about three or four pages. I was convinced that we could not depend on the religious or moral forces in Birmingham. If a breakthrough was to occur in the South's biggest and baddest city, some thrust needed to be made that would influence the ebb and flow of finance. Thus, the targets selected were primary, second, and tertiary with the presumption that the power structure would use everything in their arsenal to discourage a strong movement.

The early marches were symbolic of the nature of our Movement. City Hall was designated as the site of our prayer meetings for racial reconciliation. As we predicted and expected, "Bull" Connor played into the Movement's hands by displaying an obsession to keep demonstrators from reaching City Hall. The rest is history. The use of dogs and fire hoses, the D-Day and D-Day plus two children's marches orchestrated primarily by James Bevel, Andrew Young and Dorothy Cotton caused the commerce and industry of the South's largest city to grind to a virtual standstill. The economic boycott which was ninety-six percent effective, paralyzed the economy of downtown Birmingham. To the credit of the business community, they reached out to Movement leaders and over a period of two days crafted a truce that called a halt to the massive demonstrations on the Friday before Mother's Day in May.

The bombing of the Gaston Motel and the Reverend A. D. King's home were vain attempts to upset the hard-won agreement that set the path for a new era in Birmingham's history. As the architect of the Birmingham campaign, it has been satisfying to me to have received two keys to the city, one from a white mayor and one from a mayor of African ancestry.

The central historical significance of the Birmingham movement was alluded to earlier: Birmingham became the *germ-center of a human rights struggle that would claim international attention and forever change the landscape of both social and political demographics of the entire South.*

That is to say that Birmingham does not stand alone; Birmingham made Selma possible! The two movements, one social, altered with the public accommodations bill, the social demographics of the South. Segregation by custom and legal fiat was completely dismantled. The Selma March swung the nation's attention to the fundamental right of a democracy, the unfettered right to vote!

The Voting Rights bill changed the political demographics of the South forever. It freed whites politically as much as it did blacks.

These two occurrences, joined at the hip as Siamese twins, changed forever the social and political landscape of the Deep South where intermarriage was once illegal and no person of African ancestry had ever voted in Sunflower County, Mississippi. Birmingham killed segregation and Selma committed the body. The compelling reality is that there could have been no Selma had there not been a Birmingham. It was the sheer power of Birmingham that convinced John F. Kennedy to make a 180 degree turn on the issue of civil rights. In January, the president of the United States declared his earnest view that no additional civil rights legislation was needed. In June of the same year, on network television and radio, he made an impassioned plea for the nation to make this moral decision. The result was the introduction of what became the 1964 Public Accommodations bill. The passage of that bill established the King movement as an authentic American revolution and SCLC as a legitimate player in the pantheon of civil rights giants.

Thus, SCLC's leadership in the Selma campaign was unquestioned. Nonviolence's full credibility was firmly established in the Birmingham campaign and the shadow of King's leadership was immeasurably lengthened with the awarding of the Nobel Prize for Peace in December, 1964. Overnight the movement had become internationalized and Birmingham had played a critical role in this new dimension of race relations politics in America.

6

REMEMBERING THE BIRMINGHAM MOVEMENT

Fred L. Shuttlesworth

This is an unusual situation when cities begin honoring the criminal. I confess to being a great criminal when it comes down to trying to get rid of segregation. I am a notorious outlaw. I have absolutely no empathy in my heart for segregation. I hope, my friends, that in this beginning, in this city, that has been so widely and diversely divided, there can come to pass what Martin Luther King talked about as the beloved community. Here you don't have to love me because I'm black or white, just love me because I'm God's child. Love me because God made us all. Love me and I'll love you. God knew what he was doing and nobody had to tell him. And if God could hold creation at bay and in balance without clashing and killing us, God also can help us to learn how to get along one with one another. One of the tragedies of segregation days was that the people who might have wanted to talk to one another, couldn't. I should have met attorney David Vann long before the demonstrations. Lola Hendricks, and all of us who just wanted to be free, should have been able to sit down anywhere, in this room or in another place, and talk with others freely. You must remember that in this building, "Bull" Connor arrested Senator Glenn Taylor of Idaho in 1948. Later, Mrs. Eleanor Roosevelt took a seat in the middle of the church to protest that arrest and the only reason Mr. Connor didn't arrest her was that she was the wife of the president of the United States. "Bull" was a crazy politician. I'm glad we took off his horns and made a steer out of him.

I'm thankful to God for several things. I'm glad that writers see some things and what they don't see, God sees. I'm glad that God's Son emphasized one word that would make and keep people free, and that word is: truth. "You shall know the truth and truth shall make you free."

Marjorie White wanted to use those words, "Birmingham Revolutionaries" to title this symposium. I thought that they didn't fit with our strategy. Although we were "revolutionary" in a sense, we were more evolutionary. The first pose for the statue of me that now stands in front of the Birmingham Civil Rights Institute included a big fist. When I understood that, I said to Mayor Arrington who was commissioning the statue for the City, "That can't be me with that fist. We had our hands open, extending the hand of friendship and fellowship as our non-violent will to negotiate." The ober-dictum for peace in this world is, "Come now and let us reason together." When people can learn to do that, then we will not have to fight against each other.

Anne Braden, a Louisville, Kentucky newspaper woman and civil rights activist, asked me one time, when she didn't know as much about me as she does now, "What would one of your chief wishes be if you had your wish with Mr. Connor?" "You don't seek the humanness," I often said to Mr. Connor. I called him "Mr. Connor" because non-violence strains and stresses itself least. It is nice to be nice to your enemies. But he just called himself "Bull" and that's why we had to do the rough stuff and get his steer horns.

Ann Braden also asked, "What would you like if you had your way? I said to her, "I would like the day to come when Mr. Connor and I and others can just sit down and talk just like men to men, women to women and people to people."

I thank you for being here. Thank you for supporting the Birmingham Historical Society in trying to move at the truth. I said to Marjorie White, "Just make it true. Don't worry about making me or the movement look good. Just tell it like it happened." Somebody said to me, as we were driving by my statue at the Institute, "How do you feel when you pass by that statue over there?" I said, "Well, I wasn't working for a statue." The key place where I want my name and my record is in heaven. "My witness is on high." What God writes is forever.

I'm thankful to God for allowing me to be born in the twentieth century and in that part of the twentieth century that could work with Reverend King, Reverend Walker, Reverend Abernathy, Reverend Steele and all the people of the Birmingham movement who worked to bring change to this nation. First Timothy 1:12 states my position. The Apostle Paul said it better: "I thank Christ Jesus our Lord, who has enabled me, for he counted me faithful; putting me into this ministry." I haven't had a lot of theology like the theologians speaking at this symposium, but I had enough to understand that Paul was right when he said, "It is not I, but Christ, who lives in me."

If you wonder what made me act the fool, it was what Christ put in me, so you have to blame him. I told the Reverend Luke Beard, pastor of the Sixteenth Street Baptist Church in 1956, when he told me that the Lord told him to tell me to call off a meeting organizing the Alabama Christian Movement for Human Rights, "I won't go backwards." After Reverend Beard called me a second time, I told him, "If the Lord wants me to call it off, He'll have to come down from heaven Himself and tell me. Tell Him, don't forget to bring the nail prints in his Hands and side." This was the powerful faith of our movement that broke the back of segregation.

CONTRIBUTORS

Glenn Eskew (Ph.D., University of Georgia) is associate professor of history at Georgia State University in Atlanta. The Birmingham native has explored the local Birmingham civil rights movement in his masters, doctoral and post-doctoral studies and fellowships at the University of Georgia, Harvard University, the Albert Einstein Institute and the W. E. B. Du Bois Institute. He is the author of *But for Birmingham: The Local and the National Movements in the Civil Rights Struggle,* which won the 1999 Francis B. Simkins Award of the Southern Historical Association.

Wilson Fallin, Jr. (Ph.D., University of Alabama) is professor of history at the University of Montevallo. A scholar of the African-American church in Birmingham, he also serves as as president of the Birmingham Baptist Bible College and as the pastor of the Oak Grove Baptist Church. He is the author of *Shelter in a Storm; The African American Church in Birmingham, 1815-1963.*

Andrew Manis (Ph.D. The Southern Baptist Theological Seminary) is Lecturer in American History at Macon State College in Macon, Georgia. A native of Birmingham, he has served as professor of religion at Xavier University of Louisiana, Averett College, and Mercer University. He has authored *Southern Civil Religions in Conflict: Black and White Baptists and Civil Rights, 1947-1957* (1987) and the definitive biography titled, *A Fire You Can't Put Out: The Civil Rights Life of Birmingham's Reverend Fred Shuttlesworth.*

Aldon Morris (Ph.D. University of Michigan) has taught sociology at the University of New York, Stony Brook, the University of

Michigan and since 1988 at Northwestern University, Evanston, Illinois. Morris's prize winning 1984 publication *The Origins of the Civil Rights Movement: Black Communities Organizing for Change* is a text in civil rights and religion courses across the nation. In addition to numerous other articles, books and community service, Morris served as consultant to the *Eyes on the Prize* television documentary.

Fred L. Shuttlesworth (B.S. Alabama State College), one of the most unsung heroes of the civil rights movement, was the central civil rights leader in Birmingham from 1956 through the 1960s. As founder and president of the Alabama Christian Movement for Human Rights, he challenged segregation and Birmingham Commissioner of Public Safety Eugene T. "Bull" Connor. He set the stage for and participated in the historic 1963 demonstrations. Shuttlesworth was also one of the founding members of the Southern Christian Leadership Conference. Since 1961 he has served as the pastor of the Greater New Light Baptist Church in Cincinnati, Ohio.

Wyatt T. Walker (D.Min., Colgate Rochester Divinity School) is Senior Minister of the Canaan Baptist Church of Christ, New York, New York. Walker served from 1959 to 1964 as chief of staff of Martin Luther King, Jr.'s Southern Christian Leadership Conference. In 1963 he served as the architect of Project C, the plan for the Birmingham marches of April and May, 1963. He is the author of numerous books, most notably *"Somebody's Calling My Name": Black Sacred Music and Social Change.*

Marjorie L. White (M.Phil., Yale University) is Director of the Birmingham Historical Society. She organized the "Birmingham Revolutionaries" symposium, and edited *A Walk to Freedom: The Rev. Fred Shuttlesworth and the Alabama Christian Movement for Human Rights.* In addition, she has written or co-edited numerous publications on Birmingham architecture and history.